RUBIES
& *Pearls*

ONE HUNDRED DAYS FOR CHANGE

Devotions to develop a heart for spiritual awareness, involvement, and activism

Dr. Lee Ann B. Marino, Ph.D., D.Min., D.D.

RUBIES & Pearls
ONE HUNDRED DAYS FOR CHANGE

Dr. Lee Ann B. Marino, Ph.D., D. Min., D.D.

Published by:

Remnant Words

(An imprint of The Righteous Pen Publications Group)
www.righteouspenpublications.com

Unless otherwise noted, all Scriptures taken from The Expanded Bible. Copyright © 2011 by Thomas Nelson. Used by permission. All rights reserved.

Scriptures marked **GNT are from the Good News Translation in Today's English Version- Second Edition** Copyright © 1992 by American Bible Society. Used by Permission.

All passages marked KJV are taken from the **Holy Bible, Authorized King James Version,** Public Domain.

Book Classification: Books > Religion & Spirituality > Worship & Devotion > Devotionals.

ISBN: 1-940197-46-5
13-Digit: 978-1-940197-46-3

Printed in the United States of America.

Never doubt that a small group of thoughtful,
committed people can change the world.
Indeed, it is the only thing that ever has.
- Margaret Mead[1]

- TABLE OF CONTENTS -

Looking at our Devotions to Develop a Heart of Spiritual Awareness, Involvement, and Activism

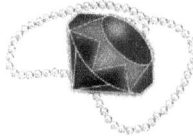

ubies and pearls are considered jewels of immeasurable beauty, worn by the most elegant and classiest of women. Rubies exist naturally from pink to dark red, but we often associate them with the typical dark red shade, one that suggests life, vigor, willpower, leadership, and courage. Rubies get their red color from chromium, an element found in them. What we don't know about the ruby is that it is the third hardest mineral found in nature, behind diamonds and moissanite. In nature, they hold their own, standing up to the toughest of treatment. They don't just represent beauty; they also represent strength. They are considered one of the four precious stones, and they contain their own natural imperfections, which separate them from fake stones. They are hard to find and among some of the rarest gemstones in the world.[1]

Pearls are created within mollusks to create a defense against an irritant or parasite within the creature. This means that pearls are a part of the immune system of mollusks, something that evolves to ward off something deemed harmful.[2] While we look at pearls as beautiful aspects of creation (and they certainly are), their calcium carbonate formation tells a much deeper story than just mere beauty. They reflect defense against attack, formation of beauty from the difficult, and the promise that we are given defenses by God to protect us from those things that seek to harm us.

Put the rubies and pearls together and you have strength and beauty, defense against invaders and substance, and purpose and dignity. This is much like our process to conform to God's image as we address the social issues in this world, becoming more of who He desires us to be.

As a Christian minister, social activism has always played an important role in my life. I don't believe it is possible to be a leader of the Gospel and not put the "social Gospel" to work. By "social Gospel" I'm talking about the purpose and work of the Gospel in an interpersonal, tangible form, one that gives us the ability to bring the work of Christ to life in our own lives and ministries. It is the Gospel lived out in a social way, with a social call, that influences and impacts people on a thoroughly social level. Yes, God calls us to preach, but God also calls us to serve. If we never apply the work of the Gospel on a social level, we are missing a key element in Gospel proclamation and living. Ministry is not just about preaching in church. Christianity is not about wearing T-shirts with Bible verses on them or watching Christian movies. As believers, we are called to become Christ-like, exemplifying His values in our every move and impacting lives.

In His ministry, Jesus was very interpersonal. He reached people where they were and sought to stand for justice and integrity. He proclaimed a new day to the poor and reprimanded those who exploited others. Jesus' message of change wasn't just spiritual; He also proclaimed a shake-up in the world, the promise of a coming Kingdom where all the problems we see around us will be no more. This doesn't mean that Jesus did not attend to things right in front of Him. While He was here, He did what needed to be done. Thus, while we are here, waiting for Him to come, we, likewise, do what needs to be done.

Social change starts with us. It starts when we change our thinking, our mindsets, our attitudes and concepts about what it means to be church and what it means when we face the issues of this world. It does not have to be political, nor does it have to be governmental. It just must be Kingdom. If we are willing to overcome our issues, we can be that much more powerful and effective. For the next 100 days, we are laying the foundation of that change, in little ways…step by step…to become the advocates, the doers, the ministers, and ultimately the Christians who step up when all hope seems to be lost elsewhere.

- DAY 1 -
Be not Afraid

So don't worry [fear], because I am with you. Don't be afraid [dismayed], because I am your God. I will make you strong [strengthen you] and will help you; I will support [uphold] you with My right hand that saves you [or righteous right hand; a symbol of power to save and protect; Ex. 15:6; Ps. 63:8].
(Isaiah 41:10)

• DAILY READING: PSALM 34:1-14

Have you ever stepped back and realized that fear is a programmed response to circumstances? When all of us were growing up, we were told to be afraid of things. This was especially true for us, as girls. Any time we wanted to step out, step up, or do something new, we were met with a chorus of voices that told us, for one reason or another, that we needed to be afraid. We were taught to fear our entire world: strangers, men, boys, other girls who weren't really our friends, the dark, the night, walking anywhere alone, people with candy, child abductors, rapists, drugs, alcohol, and the invisible enemies that we heard about, lurking to and fro, but didn't really know who they were or how to identify them.

Those who were a part of our world and who taught us these mechanisms of fear thought they were helping us to make it to adulthood. They recognized the very real dangers that exist in this world, and they didn't want us to go through our lives thinking that we can avoid them. They wanted us to be prepared in case one of these different things besieged us, so we could handle it – and ourselves – without being harmed or hurt.

The problem with the fear-based thinking we grew up with is that it doesn't just extend to one area of our lives. Growing up with the idea that we need to be afraid of things all the time equates to other social conditions and complications. We take protecting ourselves to a whole new level, allowing fear to keep us reserved and in a box, using those

3

fears instilled within us to protect us from harm to protect us from social opposition and discomfort.

So many of us are afraid of so many things. We are afraid of retaliation if we speak up about wrongdoing we see. We're afraid that our friends or families will alienate us. We're afraid of being stopped by the authorities and something routine turning into something vile. We're afraid we will lose our jobs. We're afraid others will judge us for something we say or do. If you step back and think about it, we spend a great deal of our lives in fear.

This is why God has told us "Be not afraid" so many times in the Bible. We need God's reminder that fear of life, of new experiences, of new people, and of standing up and speaking out is not a part of our inheritance as Christians. As believers, we should never feel we have to fear doing the right thing will cost us more than we can handle. In every situation, we either believe that God is there for us, or we do not. Instead of focusing on the things that scare us, every one of us should take the time to focus on the things God has told us to do – and leave it at that.

- DAILY DISCIPLINE: THINK OF AN EVERYDAY FEAR YOU HAVE, AND MAKE AN ACTION PLAN TO CONQUER IT.

- DAY 2 -
So Great a Company of Women

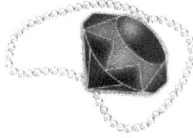

THE LORD GAVE THE COMMAND, AND A GREAT ARMY
[OR COMPANY OF WOMEN] TOLD THE NEWS.
(PSALM 68:11)

- DAILY READING: JUDGES 4:1-24

*I*f you were anything like me, you grew up in a church that told you women didn't have an equal voice or place with the men. While men were able to be ordained as pastors, bishops, deacons, and serve in all sorts of elaborate roles, women were not allowed this right within the church's doctrine. This meant that no matter how much they might have told us we had every right to be there in the church and that it was our church, too, there was something in that statement that gave us girls a double message. We might have believed it was our church, but if we were to remain a part of that church, there were going to be things we would never become nor have the right to aspire.

People who believe that women have a subordinate place to men in the church have not been properly taught to interpret the Scriptures and understand the bottom-line revelation that despite what culture may teach us, there is neither male nor female in Christ. This is because God not only created all of us for potential, He created all of us with purpose and gifts...and that includes His women, as well as His men.

As women, we are probably not aware of the true reality we have as agents of His change, women of true purpose and destiny, gifted and uniquely created in God's image. We have been given the same dominion and authority as men have, and believe it or not, God can call us, too! In fact, call us, He does. We might not be attuned to hear His call to us, and we might try to run from it when it is there, but there are those of us whom God does call in this day, this hour, to do the right thing at the right time, just for Him.

If, as the Bible states, there is a great company of women, that automatically means there are many of us. It also means we move in a unison, a unity, for His greater purpose. While we might be a group who "proclaims the good news," the way that each of us is called to do that varies slightly, that the message might be reached by everyone, in all parts of the world. Issued with a certain militancy to it, our work as a company of women means we will face opposition, be in situations to fight an enemy who disguises himself in ways we would never expect and be ready to engage in that fight when opportunity arises.

Yet, if we want to be an effective company, that means we need to learn how to work together, especially with our sisters in the Lord. We all know women have a reputation for not getting things done because they are too busy gossiping or backbiting one another. It is our day and our hour to change this tide and move as a strong, purposed unit. The sooner we do this, the sooner we will see the change we want in the world.

- DAILY DISCIPLINE: MINDFULLY REFRAIN FROM GOSSIP OF ANY SORT FOR 24 HOURS.

- DAY 3 -
We are Here to Serve

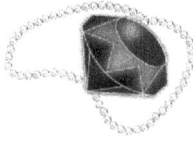

IF I, YOUR LORD AND TEACHER, HAVE WASHED YOUR FEET,
YOU ALSO SHOULD WASH EACH OTHER'S FEET.
(JOHN 13:14)

- DAILY READING: JOHN 13:1-20

Most of us have attended a foot washing service at some point in our lives. What do you remember about it? If you are like way too many women, you probably remember the whole focus of the event revolving around how modest the women should dress. If people were going to be down on the floor washing feet, the church's major concern was for the women to wear a long enough skirt so no one could see up our dress, and the men should not wash the women's feet of the church (even though no one would fuss over the women washing the men's feet). In efforts to maintain certain codes of chastity, we spent all our time worrying about what might happen between people intimately instead of learning about the significance of the foot washing ceremony.

In ancient cultures (and in some parts of the Middle East, even today), people either wore sandals, other minimal footwear, or no shoes, at all. In dry, dusty conditions, this becomes both unsanitary and unhealthy. Shoes were removed upon entry to the house, and it was the position of the servant to wash the feet of guests prior to eating, because meals were traditionally served on the floor.

Having to be the slave that washed the feet of others was considered the lowest position of low positions in a household. It was a job that nobody wanted (can we blame them?). The level of humility associated with it was associated with personal demoralization and was something nobody wanted for themselves in life.

Yet washing feet was still a job that somebody had to do, because it had to be done. Considered lowly or not, it was something that needed doing because not doing it could cause people to get sick, a home to be dirty, or the spread of disease. It had to be done, and when the time came to do it, humble or not, it was a requirement of each and every household.

For our Savior to assume this position and wash the feet of His disciples – men who, within the next few days, most of whom would abandon Him in His darkest hour – is most relevant to us. We don't want to adopt the position of servant, especially to those we deem to be against us or who we do not like, but that is exactly what our Savior modeled for us. In His love, He loved those who listened to His teaching and followed Him enough to serve them, to perform the tasks deemed the lowest of the low on their behalf.

Love serves. If we say we believe in service, then we should be serving others, whether we like them or not, whether we want to be their friends or not, whether we are related to them or not, and whether we think they are worthy of what we do for them. Our Savior set the bar, and set it high, just by humbling Himself enough to sit low, look up at others, and wash their feet.

- DAILY DISCIPLINE: DO SOMETHING GOOD FOR SOMEONE THAT YOU DO NOT LIKE.

- DAY 4 -

Blessed are Those Who Mourn

THEY ARE BLESSED WHO GRIEVE [MOURN], FOR GOD WILL COMFORT THEM [THEY WILL BE COMFORTED; THE PASSIVE VERB IMPLIES GOD AS SUBJECT]. (MATTHEW 5:4)

- DAILY READING: DEUTERONOMY 34:1-12

My mom tells me about the days when people experienced a death in the family and their friends, neighbors, co-workers, and fellow church members showed up with food, flowers, babysitting services, housekeeping services, and general comfort in order to offer their condolences for that loved one's passing. The friends, neighbors, and members of the community were the ones who helped that person regain a sense of normalcy as they allowed them the time they needed to grieve while attending to the practical needs that seemed impossible to attain. Their grief, the place they were at in a state of mourning, was all-encompassing, and was too much to bear by themselves. The presence of others and their caring silence, offering practical help and a listening ear, was more than enough to help those in mourning come to a place where they were ready and prepared to attend to the issues of living, once again.

I don't see a lot of this in my day. I don't see many people go out of their way to help others who are mourning or help other people in a practical way. When someone dies, there might be people who stand on the sidelines with apologies or observations, but there aren't many people who are willing to step up and do something to help those who are mourning. Instead, I hear a lot of words spoken when people are in states of mourning. Most of those statements, I believe, are said because we don't know what else to say to people and we think that a word of hope equates to a word of comfort. The truth is that in most instances, it does not. When people are dealing with serious loss or are at points in their lives that have brought them to a place where the only thing they can do is mourn...mourn for the person they have lost...mourn for the thing they have lost...mourn for the sense of community and justice they have lost...or mourn for the part of themselves that they have lost.

In moments like these, hope hurts. It hurts to think that there is a world out there that will come up and knock on the hearts, minds, and lives of people who are hurting. It sounds like an insensitive wound, something that is being said to try and make someone feel guilty for their mourning or for the place they find themselves in. There's a reason the Bible's injunction is to "comfort those who are mourning," not "encourage those who are mourning." At some points of our lives, encouragement isn't the answer, but comfort is.

Thus, when you are confronted with someone in mourning, the answer is to be a comforting, healing presence, one that reminds them God is there with them and so are you. It's not, in that moment, about the future, about tomorrow, about the bigger picture: it's about that one person, their situation, their immediate need to know you love them, and God does, too.

- DAILY DISCIPLINE: SEND A CONDOLENCE CARD TO SOMEONE WHO HAS LOST A LOVED ONE.

- Day 5 -

Too Young to Get Married

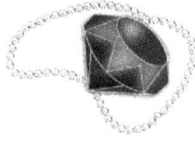

"Later when I passed by you and looked at you, I saw that [behold] you were old enough for love. So I spread My robe [the corner of my garment; Deut. 22:30; Ruth 3:9] over you and covered your nakedness. I also made a promise [swore; made a vow] to you and entered into an agreement [covenant; treaty; Ex. 19:5] with you so that you became Mine, says the Lord God."
(Ezekiel 16:8)

- Daily Reading: Ezekiel 13:1-14

Most in western nations think it appalling for girls to be deprived of a childhood. We love the idea of watching girls grow up and enjoying their days, whether they are girly-girls or tomboys, because the art of childhood play is essential to forming creativity, imagination, and a life-long love for all things curious. In fact, in some instances, we have tried so hard to make sure they have a childhood that we have started spoiling our children. As with all things, extremes are never good, but there is an extreme of life that we do not know much about if we haven't learned about it.

For millions of girls around the world, there is no such thing as childhood or play. From the time they are born or very, very young, they are thrust into a world that seeks to prepare them for marriage. They are pulled out of school, taught how to keep house, and even taught to endure things such as physical beatings or emotional abuses from their future husbands, who are selected for them by their parents. These girls are literally sold to a family that offers them the best deal, selling their daughters as soon as they reach puberty to men who may be much older, who often do not love or care for them, or who may already have other wives. Their feelings do not matter. Their wishes do not matter. In their adulthood, they spend their lives in a form of alienated domestic slavery which makes it so they cannot empower themselves or escape, thus they stay out of fear...and go on to

11

perpetuate the cycle.

Our culture tends to romanticize the notion of marriage and family to a point where we forget there are many in the world who do not feel the same way about it. Their experience of marriage does not reflect love or romance, but time-honored traditions that hurt our young girls and keep them violated and dejected. By violating girls in this most sacred way, it makes understanding of God, of His love for us, something foreign. These are women who do not know of the beautiful type that we have in our relationship with God; He as our Lord and we as His bride.

As women, we need to stop turning a blind eye to the cultural traditions that are in our midst that kill or hurt girls. Child marriage is an obvious one, but there are other ways we give our girls the message that God isn't really for them. Whenever we are partial with boys in church when it comes to preparing them for ministry or preaching, we are saying that God is for those boys, and not for those girls. Whenever we are constantly giving girls messages about growing up so they can get married and have children while we tell the boys that they are created for great things, we are telling those girls that God isn't for them. Whenever we uphold cultural values, encouraging girls to be "pure" and boys to do whatever, we are telling girls that God is unjust.

We need to care that girls are being married off, as common property in our world today. We also need to care that we are telling girls everywhere that they don't really matter, even in western culture.

- DAILY DISCIPLINE: RESEARCH AND CREATE A PRESENTATION ABOUT CHILD MARRIAGE IN THE WORLD TODAY.

- DAY 6 -
Commitment

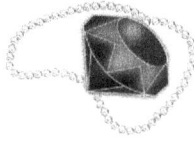

IF YOU MAKE A PROMISE [VOW] TO GOD, DON'T BE SLOW TO KEEP [DELAY TO FULFILL] IT. GOD IS NOT HAPPY [FOR THERE IS NO PLEASURE] WITH FOOLS, SO GIVE GOD WHAT YOU PROMISED [FULFILL WHAT YOU HAVE VOWED].
(ECCLESIASTES 5:4)

- DAILY READING: LEVITICUS 5:4-13

*I*t's a universal complaint among leaders that it's very hard to get people to make – and keep – their commitments. Years ago, I remember someone saying that if 75% of people who committed to doing something actually followed through, it was a lot. Nowadays I sit with other ministers who are ready to pull their hair out because even if a commitment is made, the anticipation must be there that someone – or no one – will follow through to see it finished (if they even show up).

It's a dirty little secret in the church world (as well as advocacy groups) that the volunteers, involvements, and group commitment that led movements (such as the Civil Rights Movement or the Feminist Movement) to victory is often lacking in our general substructures. There are often people with good ideas or interesting visions, but because people are vying to be in charge, get noticed, get credit, or get too busy, those ideas and visions never seem to materialize. They get lost in the haze of everyday life that people seem to have a hard time handling and whatever the bigger picture is that requires that involvement fades in the background.

People of God should not be people who falter on their commitments. It is not acceptable to use family involvements to avoid being involved in the church and in the community. Having families is not new. People who were a part of community service and involved had them in years past...so the excuse that we are too busy with our families indicates we are, literally, too busy with them. If our excuse is work, working and having jobs is not new, either, and people who were a part of community service and involvement in years past also had jobs…so the excuse that we are too busy with our jobs indicates we are, literally, too busy with them, too. Whatever our excuse, whatever what we say to try and justify ourselves is just that…an excuse…and excuses prove that we know our lack of commitment is both wrong and unchristian.

A big part of what separates Christianity from other belief systems is a willingness for believers to be hands-on and get dirty when it counts. All of us want God to do great and awesome things for us in our lives, but we don't want to get dirty or hands-on in the process. Being a Christian is not about being elitist! We aren't here to change the world by adopting its pomp and circumstance, having other people worship us and setting ourselves up as grand masters. We are here to be involved, to be committed to things that are bigger than ourselves, our families, our need to make money or be promoted, and to be people who stand behind our word and God's Word so things around us will change.

Until we get our heads around a right understanding of Christianity, we will keep faltering on our commitments. If we believe what we say has power, then our yes must mean yes and our no mean no…and anything else in between displays a lack of true commitment. If you've said you are involved, then get involved all the way!

- DAILY DISCIPLINE: KEEP YOUR COMMITMENTS!

- DAY 7 -

Combat Wrong by Being Yourself

WE MUST NOT BECOME TIRED [OR DISCOURAGED] OF DOING GOOD.
WE WILL RECEIVE OUR HARVEST OF ETERNAL LIFE AT THE RIGHT [OR IN DUE]
TIME IF WE DO NOT GIVE UP.
(GALATIANS 6:9)

• DAILY READING: ROMANS 1:10-17

Everywhere we look, we see strains of wrong all around us. Whether it's racism, sexism, homophobia, violence, abuse, superiority, intimidation, economic depression, or brutality, we are in a world surrounded by wrong. Wrong, in all its various forms, is so ingrained within our society, we don't even tend to notice the millions of ways that wrong permeates our lives. It happens every day, unnoticed, and people experience the sting of wrong's injustices in silence, as people fail to recognize what has been done to them.

After a particularly bad siege of deaths due to brutality, bigotry and violence, I was asked by my spiritual daughter, what can we do about it? I replied to her that I think it is important we live according to our values and that we are ourselves with other people. Not too long before, I heard some stories about people going out of their way to grab someone at a gas pump and apologize for all the things that their race might be feeling about what was going on within society. While the woman might have thought she was doing something to help, what she was doing, in a weird way, was profiling that woman. Instead of just being herself, instead of just being kind and exemplifying God's love, she had to try and do something that sounded good, but in reality, caused the woman that she stopped to feel weird and creepy.

I have long said that treating all people with respect is something my mother taught me, and living by that principle honors my mother as well as honors the kind of person I want to be. Those of us who know the proper way to behave with other people need to do just that. Instead of trying to create moments that make people uncomfortable because they force issues on them, we need to make a point to be people who do the right thing and who by doing the right thing, create moments of comfort and empathy with all people, those who are like we are and those who are different from us.

When wrong things happen and we know about them, our first inclination is to do something about them. We want to march, we want to boycott, maybe we want to write to politicians, or maybe we want something to be done within our community. There's nothing wrong with any of this, but the catch to it all is that it does not heal the hearts of those who have been wounded. If we want to be people who want to change wrong, we need to live as people who believe in right rather than wrong. We need to let our conduct be known to all men, showing love to those who have been wronged and showing the strangers we meet true care as they pass through our lives.

We can make a difference. They used to tell us, if we want to change the world, start with yourself. This is true, in more than one way, because we can most definitely change the world if we are willing to do the right thing for other people, just by being ourselves, even when no one else is willing to do it.

- DAILY DISCIPLINE: MAKE SOMEONE'S DAY BETTER BY BEING A BLESSING TO THEM.

- DAY 8 -
A Friend Loves at All Times

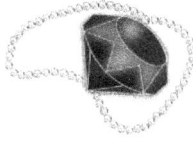

A FRIEND LOVES YOU ALL THE TIME, AND A BROTHER HELPS IN
[IS BORN FOR A] TIME OF TROUBLE.
(PROVERBS 17:17)

- DAILY READING: 2 SAMUEL 1:17-27

*I*t might seem odd in a book on activism and unity to find a devotional about friendship. Friendship is a topic that one might think of for a devotional on practical living or something of that nature. What we don't consider, however, is that our alliances and bonds in friendship teach us a lot about unity in the Body of Christ. How we interact with our friends and the type of bonds and friendships that we pursue tell both ourselves and others who we want to be as people and how well we can get along with others who are around us.

I don't think it's a big secret in church that we have a serious unity problem. We have this problem because we don't understand the principles behind connecting to other people for the purpose of working together. We place human questions and concerns into the discussion about unity: who is going to be in charge? How are we going to get everything done? Who is going to get the credit? What are we to do if things go awry on us? These questions show us that we are not as advanced as we might like to think we are, and that while we can be spiritual on our own, we have not learned how to be spiritual when we are with other people.

Our friendships are a great training ground for learning how to unite with other people because friendship forces us, in a way many do not consider, to recognize what is most important to us in our lives. Who our friends are say a lot about us and a lot about those that we find ourselves able to get along with. Friendship proves that as much as we might be disagreeable in certain situations, we are able to work with others as God works on us, one step at a time.

The principle that a "friend loves at all times" might sound easy, but in reality, it's not. Friends aren't people we are expected to love; they are people we choose to love and choose to serve, wanting to enhance our own lives and theirs in the process. We arrange outings or trips, social events, and time spent together. We make things work with our friends, sorting out differences of opinion, fights, disagreements, and the ways our lives may vary from one another. Despite these differences and the times when we don't get along, if we always love our friends, we press through these challenges and come out the other side. Friends teach us about love, and they teach us how to love.

Friends are the starting ground for us to learn how to love other people in our lives. Of all the things in the Bible that relate to love, it is only friends that are spoken of as loving "at all times." Love remains a central tenant of Christianity, even if we aren't hearing about it regularly. We learn how to always love, how to consider others, how to deal with our disagreements and how to be there for other people as we establish ourselves as friendly and make friends with others. Love your friends. Appreciate them. It's not easy to replace those who are tried and true.

- DAILY DISCIPLINE: TAKE A FRIEND OF YOURS OUT FOR LUNCH OR DINNER TO SHOW YOUR APPRECIATION TO THEM.

- DAY 9 -
I was Hungry and You Fed Me

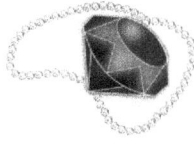

[FOR; BECAUSE] I WAS HUNGRY, AND YOU GAVE ME FOOD...
(MATTHEW 25:35)

- DAILY READING: MATTHEW 14:13-21

Those of us who lived through the 1980s probably remember the graphic images of Somalian starvation broadcast on the news through our television sets night after night. It tore at the hearts of many Americans who couldn't believe war, power, and control could cause people to disregard human lives in such an obvious way. The people suffered, children suffered, families suffered, and the devastation of starvation caused deaths many, many times over.

The catch with world hunger is that it doesn't just live on the news in the 1980s. The truth about world hunger is that over 795 million people – approximately one in every nine people in the world – do not have enough to eat. Approximately 60% of the world's hungry are women, and nearly half of all childhood deaths in children under five years of age are due to poor nutrition. Every ten seconds, a child dies from hunger-related disease.[3] Many people in the world go without proper food and nourishment because they don't have access to necessary resources to feed themselves.

I've been asked as to why God doesn't do something about starvation in the world. People recognize it as a source of intense suffering, which is undeniable if we look at the statistics with caring hearts and observant eyes. The truth is that God already has done something about starvation in this world, and that answer is to provide necessary resources so people can eat. It is man's inhumanity to man and thirst for power that causes an unequitable dispersing of those resources, thus causing starvation. The game of food and feeding others has become a dominant game: the one who controls the most resources automatically wins. The inequities in this world do not prove God to be inhumane or uncaring but call out to us as a people who are in desperate need to step up and do something to better the life of someone else.

The Bible encourages us to see the hungry are fed in a literal sense, offering food to the hungry that will satisfy hunger and erase issues of malnutrition. There are many ways this can be accomplished: food outreaches, church meals, food banks, feeding a hungry neighbor, buying groceries for someone you know needs food, and distribution of good food that might otherwise be thrown out. At the same time, the Bible is teaching us something deeper; that Christians should be opposed to political powers and programs that use starvation to enforce political controls. We should stand for the concept of a living wage, safe working conditions, and the right of individuals to provide for themselves and their families without government control or interference.

On a more basic level, the Bible is telling us we should be aware of what we have and be willing to make the sacrifice every now and then to help someone out who doesn't have enough to eat themselves, because doing such is a lasting witness in providing for need.

- DAILY DISCIPLINE: DONATE FOOD TO A LOCAL FOOD BANK.

- DAY 10 -

The Social Call of the Apostle: Diversity

To those who are weak [in faith; 8:7–13], I became weak so I could win the weak. I have become all things to all people so I could save some of them in any way possible.
(1 CORINTHIANS 9:22)

- DAILY READING: 2 CORINTHIANS 5:11-21

Many are unaware that all the five-fold ministry offices are not just works that relate to spirituality. The five-fold ministry offices also carry with them different social calls, all of which relate to the way in which different interpersonal issues are addressed within the Body of Christ. This shows us that interest in the way people interact (which is the heart of what being social is about) is as important to God as anything else, and that when it comes to our stand as Christians, the church is a powerful training ground for bringing different groups of people together who are called to focus on certain key issues that relate to our spiritual understanding.

In the instance of the apostle, the social call that we have is diversity. As an apostle myself, I recognize the relevance we have as carriers of the "New Covenant," a word that is to be brought to all people, no matter who they are or where they might be in the world. When we talk about becoming "all things to all people" we are talking about the very heart of an intercultural, integrated church that is not divided by the same social, economic, and political lines that often divide society. Here, in church, we are to represent something new and different, and the first step to doing that is to embrace the principle of diversity within our own lives and ministries.

Several years ago, I was on the phone with a minister who was admittedly gay and living with another man, even though they were not legally married (as gay marriage wasn't legal in the United States yet). I was a minister who desperately wanted to "fit in" with the constituencies I felt could help launch my ministry, and that meant I

21

didn't want to be associated with the "wrong people." This was an individual who, on account of being gay and out, would have been considered as such. It didn't help that he was an annoying person who was completely full of himself and never stopped talking. Well, me being me, all I wanted to do was get off the phone and go do something else, and he wouldn't stop his endless parade of prattle. I kept praying to God to get me off the phone, and then I got mad when God didn't cause some sort of miracle to make the way off it. The Lord, instead, spoke to me that day on that call – "I am teaching you how to become all things to all people."

It never occurred to me that there might come a time when I might work with the LGBTQ+ community (as I do now) or that God was calling me to embrace a sense of diversity beyond my comfort zone, which was, by most standards, already pretty diverse. His words certainly weren't what I wanted to hear, but it was definitely what I needed to hear. We can't bring salvation to the world if we dictate who deserves it, and when. Being able to work with different groups of people, whether we like it all the time or not and whether we always agree with them is a key aspect to apostolic ministry. As the apostles learn how to do it, they, in turn, are better able to teach the church how to embrace diversity in their ranks.

- DAILY DISCIPLINE: RECOGNIZE THE WORK OF AN APOSTLE IN PUBLIC BY THANKING THEM FOR THEIR SERVICE IN THE KINGDOM.

- DAY 11 -
Bind Up the Brokenhearted

...He has sent me to comfort [bind up] those whose hearts are broken...
(ISAIAH 61:1)

- DAILY READING: PSALM 147:1-6

roken-heartedness is never a topic that we like to approach because it signifies intense pain. It represents times in our lives where something has come along that is so deeply painful, it threatens the very core of our being and our ability to live. They might be things that others look over and tell us to "get over" or to "move past it already," but they have shaken us up so bad, they don't seem to be things that are consolable. When someone is brokenhearted, they are beyond easy consolation, and beyond the comfort that we see in different stages of mourning. Because the loss is so intense, someone is uncertain of how they can ever go forward and live normally without something again.

There are many who don't think the experience of being heartbroken is real or something to take seriously. The mere fact it is mentioned in Scripture and that it is apparently something as old as Biblical times tells us the brokenhearted experience is not new and is valid. It is also not something to brush off or treat lightly, as if it doesn't really matter. Whether it's a teenage girl experiencing the end of her first relationship or someone who experiences the loss of a child or of someone close to them, broken heartedness is not something to scoff at or ignore. Rather, it is something the Bible tells us we should "bind up."

Have you ever had an injury that didn't quite require stitches, but still needed a mending of sorts? Injuries like this that involve a separation (such as skin) are cleaned well and then bandaged up very good, not so tight that blood flow is constricted, but just enough so that the skin will meld together again and will heal on its own. This process is the "binding" spoke of in relation to those with a broken heart. The very imagery of a broken heart sees it in pieces, fractured and jagged, relates to what happens when something comes along in our lives that causes our life-source to break, the grounding of our realities to shatter. To put this back together, the heart must be bound: all the pieces brought together and tightly bandaged, giving the heart the proper time to heal from the hurt and shock, so that it can go on functioning, even though life may never be the same again.

Binding the broken heart occurs when we take the time to show people we care about them, showing appropriate empathy and compassion for a circumstance that has caused unspeakable pain. We treat people the way we would want to be treated in such a situation, expressing an undying love and a quiet hope for the future that cannot come into their lives through any other way. Sure, it might be easy to sit from afar on the sidelines and wish someone well, but binding the brokenhearted requires one to be up-close and personal, showing someone that even though something has changed their lives forever, that life can still be something precious and hopeful, with promises to embrace.

- DAILY DISCIPLINE: SHOW A HURTING PERSON THAT YOU CARE ABOUT THEM.

- DAY 12 -

Silencing the Ignorant

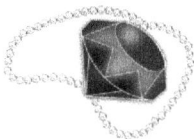

YOU TEACH THAT PERSON NOT TO [THAT HE NEED NOT] HONOR HIS FATHER
OR HIS MOTHER. YOU REJECTED [INVALIDATED; CANCELED; NULLIFIED]
WHAT GOD SAID [THE WORD OF GOD] FOR THE SAKE OF YOUR OWN RULES
[TRADITION].
(MATTHEW 15:6)

- DAILY READING: 1 PETER 2:11-17

All of us have gotten into debates with people on social media that left us scratching our heads and baffled at the level of ignorance someone displayed during the discussion. What seemed to be perfectly logical and obvious to us was clearly not that way to them, and no matter how much we seemed to present facts and information contrary to what they were saying, they insisted that they were right, often to the dissolution of the entire discussion. Right after you want to pull your hair out, you all walk away, often not wanting to speak ever again, and making a personal note to avoid such debates and arguments in the future.

Perhaps the greatest example of this can be displayed in the many statuses and memes that tell people not to add a certain person on Facebook because that person is a hacker, or who spread the rumors and lies that people are kidnapping and raping people at gas stations by making them smell business cards laced with a drop of ether, or who tell others not to join a certain group because it has been started by child molesters. My personal favorite are the posts that, time and time again, say Facebook is going to start charging for use at midnight on a certain day, and it was reported on the news!

None of these statuses, memes, or common urban legends have any basis in fact. Here, in this devotion, I have barely scratched the surface of the various rumors and things that circulate online which can be proven false with the most basic of research. There are many sites and verifiable news outlets that report these different things to be false, yet they circulate anyway. The reason they circulate is the same reason we deal with people who do not want to hear the most basic of facts: ignorance.

We don't like to think that we've participated in ignorance, but the truth is that we all have at some point in our lives. Hopefully we have pulled ourselves together enough to learn some facts to combat ignorance, which helps us to look at life in a different way. Now, when we deal with ignorance, we get frustrated, seeing them as unwilling to educate themselves on the issues of the day, trusting instead every news story that crosses their television set or internet feed.

People remain ignorant because it is easier to remain ignorant than it is to step out and take the chance that maybe the principles and precepts they have stood upon (their traditions) are wrong. It has become an internet tradition to live in fear of certain people or groups, or to fear new information, which echoes us back to basic principles that always relate to proper education in societies among people. As people, we need to be educated, and I am not just talking about attending school. I am talking about the consistent call to know what is going on so that we can constructively, through our actions and words, silence the ignorant traditions of men that nullify the truth.

- DAILY DISCIPLINE: MAKE SURE THAT WHAT YOU SHARE ONLINE IS TRUE BEFORE YOU SHARE IT.

- DAY 13 -
Have Pity on the Poor

BEING KIND [GRACIOUS; GENEROUS] TO THE POOR IS LIKE LENDING TO THE
LORD; HE WILL REWARD YOU FOR WHAT YOU HAVE DONE [FULLY REPAY YOU].
(PROVERBS 19:17)

- DAILY READING: DEUTERONOMY 15:7-11

*I*n the early years of Christianity, care for the poor was one of the central focuses of the faith. Reading the stories of early saints of the faith shows devoted men and women who, because of their love for Jesus Christ and their fellow man, turned their back on their wealthy, worldly lives to work among the poor in the harshest conditions imaginable. There are stories of people who sold every possession they had (very much to the chagrin of their families) and forsook power and prestige to work among the simplest of people who often had the least.

You'd be hard-pressed to find someone so committed to service in the Kingdom that they turn their backs on a life of ease and good money to serve the poor today, although it does happen from time to time. There are those in every era who feel so moved by the work of God in their lives that they want to reach out and help those who are less fortunate than they are. The reality is it is a monumental thing to take one's life and devote it to the poor in such a radical way. Forsaking all to make sure someone with less has a better life is most definitely a call, something one must hear, and answer, as they seek the Lord for ways to serve in this world.

The examples we have just discussed might be considered a little extreme, individuals whose hearts moved them to compassion and to do something that the average person is not called to do. The concept of having pity on the poor and giving to the poor, however, is something for all Christians to pursue at every point in their lives. We may not be asked of God to give up every single thing we have for the poor, but we are asked to have a certain esteem for the poor, making sure that we give to those who have less than we do on a regular basis.

Having pity doesn't mean looking down on other people like we use the word now. To have pity meant to have empathy for, to understand a situation and to do what someone could in order to raise that other person up. Too often we hear blaming remarks against poor people that imply they are responsible for their circumstances. The poor are told they are lazy, don't work or want to work, aren't willing to work hard, or are just looking for a handout. Being called to pity the poor means we stop all this rhetoric, stop judging others and their situations, and just do what is called for, instead.

The thing we don't see about giving to the poor is that doing so is a "loan" or a "lending" unto God Himself. When we give to someone who can't give back to us, the gift is between us and God, and God Himself will repay us for what we've done by blessing us in our lives. This is about more than us and others; it's also about us and God. The sooner we start giving to the poor, the sooner God will return the favor and bless us more abundantly in our lives.

- DAILY DISCIPLINE: PUT TOGETHER A SMALL HYGIENE BAG WITH TRAVEL-SIZE ITEMS AND HAND IT OUT TO A HOMELESS PERSON ASKING FOR MONEY ON THE STREET.

- DAY 14 -
Love Your Neighbor Means Love Your Neighbor

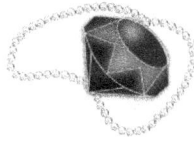

THIS ROYAL LAW [BECAUSE GOD THE KING DECREED IT, OR BECAUSE IT IS THE
SUPREME LAW] IS FOUND IN THE SCRIPTURES: "LOVE YOUR NEIGHBOR AS
YOU LOVE YOURSELF [LEV. 19:18; MATT. 22:37–40]." IF YOU
[OR IF YOU REALLY; OR IF YOU, HOWEVER,] OBEY [FULFILL; CARRY OUT]
THIS LAW, YOU ARE DOING RIGHT [WELL].
(JAMES 2:8)

- DAILY READING: GALATIANS 5:1-15

What does it mean when we tell someone that we love them? Maybe the bigger question is what does it mean when we talk about love, especially in the context of social change? We like to hear about love when it is about romance or marriage, but what happens when it's time to look at love from the perspective that doesn't sweep us off our feet or make us feel tingly and hot all over? How do we love those who don't love us back or even know us? How do we care about those who hate us?

The last paragraph had an awful lot of questions within it that truly challenge our definition of what it means to love our neighbor. Beyond a recurring theme in the Bible, being people who love and who live the love of God are also people who are called to love those it seems impossible to love: our neighbor. God doesn't just challenge us to love those who are easy to love (those who we know love us) but challenges us to love those we do not know, those we cannot imagine ever knowing, love those who do not love us, and love those who are so different from us, we could never imagine loving them in the first place.

This challenge of love means we are called to care about other people aside from ourselves. It makes us look at ourselves, examine ourselves, and embrace our own faults and our own issues so we can resolve them from a spiritual perspective. It's easy to surround ourselves with people who reflect our own values and who feel the same way that we do about things, but it's a lot harder to apply God's command to love other people when they are radically different from us. This command is to contrast a world embroiled in hate and envy, picking and choosing those who are the easiest to love as those we will keep closest to ourselves, lavishing and encouraging, while seeing the rest of the world as an enemy rather than a friend.

The truth is that the world is full of friends unmet, of people who are a part of God's creation and are the sons and daughters of God who are simply ignorant of that fact in the application of their own lives, and full of people who need to know and experience the Gospel. We won't be willing to live the way God calls – and requires us to as believers – with others if we are unwilling to love them. In love, we lay ourselves aside and all our earthly loyalties to focus on something greater, something more important that will lift others up rather than only focusing on elevating ourselves.

It amazes me to note that time and time again, no matter how many years I have in the work of ministry, it is truly love that challenges us the most and changes us the most as people. If there is only one message we can preach, only one that we can proclaim, and most importantly, only one that we can live, it is the embodiment that love can, will, and does transform and change every life that it encounters, often without speaking a verbal word.

- DAILY DISCIPLINE: MAKE A NEW FRIEND.

- DAY 15 -

Blessed are the Poor in Spirit

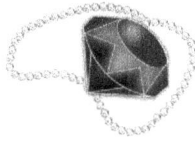

THEY ARE BLESSED [OR BLESSED ARE THOSE...; AND SO THROUGH V. 10]
WHO REALIZE THEIR SPIRITUAL POVERTY [ARE THE POOR IN SPIRIT],
FOR THE KINGDOM OF HEAVEN BELONGS TO THEM [IS THEIRS].
(MATTHEW 5:3)

• DAILY READING: ISAIAH 66:1-3

Humility is one of the most beautiful facets of the Christian faith. In humility, we recognize who we are, that in ourselves we can do nothing, but with God, we can do everything. It's no accident, then, that Jesus describes those who are "poor in spirit" as those who shall receive the Kingdom of heaven. Humility sounds powerful, noble, as a willing and total surrender to God, the One before Whom we all will stand one day.

As beautiful as a musing that humility may be in concept, it is a terrible shame that we do not honor humility as something beautiful before God and something powerful before men. Our inclinations are usually to those we see as great and powerful in the things of this world, and we are quick to want to follow such people rather than humble ourselves and follow those who are humble in turn, as well. We like the idea of capturing the world to Christ by power and influence, and don't like the idea that being so powerful and so commanding may very well be the one thing that we hold onto that keeps us out of heaven.

Being poor in spirit is a big part of living in a humble state. Those who are willing to do without anything to gain eternity are those who are poor in spirit. They have acknowledged they must empty themselves of all this world and all that they hold dear to themselves within and surrender all to the Lord, to gain all. When this is done, the Kingdom of heaven, the promise of eternity forever and ever, is what always awaits. It becomes real for those who live it as well as those who receive from it, and it becomes something not so distant or far off that

31

we have to pretend that heaven does not, in its reality, truly exist.

To be poor in spirit means to take off ourselves and put on Christ. This means far more than just putting on the mind of Christ to encourage oneself or make one feel better about themselves. It is about focusing on the things that Christ deems most important: the foundations of faith, the foundations of justice, and the principle of lifting others up, esteeming ourselves no better than them, and no less, at the same time. If we are poor in spirit, we will care, not just for ourselves, but for the world around us and seek to make the world a better place because our faith requires such of us.

It's not too much to ask that we humble ourselves before taking on work that is designed to help others and bless them in their lives. Our goal is to help people see the Kingdom of heaven at work, alive, present, so near they can touch it – not so people will notice us and praise us for the things that we do. Eternity lives within our ability to humble ourselves and touch the lives of others. We must do what we do to make that difference in their lives; nothing more, and nothing else.

- DAILY DISCIPLINE: EXAMINE YOUR OWN ARROGANCES AND HUMBLE YOURSELF BEFORE GOD.

- DAY 16 -

I was Thirsty, and You Gave Me a Drink

...I WAS THIRSTY, AND YOU GAVE ME SOMETHING TO DRINK...
(MATTHEW 25:35)

• DAILY READING: ISAIAH 55:1-7

For people who can go to their faucets and pour a glass of water from them or buy some bottled water at a convenience store, it can be hard to imagine this is not the case for everyone worldwide. The water crisis in Flint, Michigan is a sobering reality that the problem of contaminated drinking water is more than something from a bygone era. When it became world news that the drinking water in Flint, Michigan had elevated levels of lead due to old pipes and leaks in the water supply, a name and a face was given to the fact that clean water is not something promised, nor guaranteed, to people everywhere in the world. It also gave us a good, long look at the serious repercussions of contaminated water. Many residents in Flint experienced permanent health damage due to lead poisoning and others might have contracted Legionnaires' Disease because of the unclean water.

What happened in Flint, however, is only a picture of the severe shortage of access to clean water that millions of people have worldwide. It's a terrible thing to realize that approximately a billion people worldwide do not have access to safe, clean drinking water, and approximately 80% of all global diseases result from contaminated drinking water.[4] Due to governmental corruption, war, poverty, and problematic infrastructures, too many people worldwide do not have access to proper drinking water or water for washing clothes, cleaning, cooking, or bathing in the world in which we live.

It's probably hard to imagine Jesus telling us to provide drink to other people would ever become a radical statement, but the reality is in our world today, making sure people have proper water sources is an extremely revolutionary act. Because the use of poor water in water

33

supplies is often used as a means of warfare or eradication, making sure water is available to those who are thirsty, in need of proper hygiene or cleansing through water sources is a statement that is antiestablishment and equalizing for all of mankind in each and every situation.

Three-quarters of our bodies are composed of water. It only takes about three days for the body to dehydrate unto a point of death. Looking at water also means we need to examine the connection between natural and spiritual thirst. Every one of us has the longing to discover the Living Water that shall satisfy us from a spiritual perspective throughout eternity. Understanding it spiritually, however, does not mean we forget about the practical application and command to realize that a person without water or access to clean water is a person in trouble. It is a part of our Christian call to support different charitable efforts to maintain and provide clean water, pumps, wells, and other systems to those in the world who need such items so they can live, thrive, and abundantly experience the fullness of purpose that Jesus has for them.

- DAILY DISCIPLINE: DONATE BOTTLED WATER TO A CLEAN WATER PROGRAM.

- DAY 17 -
Wake up and Pay Attention!

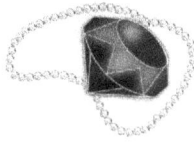

I TELL YOU THIS, AND I SAY THIS TO EVERYONE: 'BE READY
[ALERT; WATCHFUL]!
(MARK 13:37)

- DAILY READING: PSALM 94:1-23

When I was growing up, I used to hear my elders say, "The more things change, the more they stay the same." I wasn't sure what it meant as a general practice until I saw a meme on Facebook that said something to the following extent: "I don't know why we are so fascinated over the 1950s. Like, calm down! We still have milkshakes and racism." The posting made me nod in agreement in addition to thinking seriously about the message behind it. Not only have we, as a society, glorified an era of history that was severely unjust, we haven't rectified the injustices of that era through our public policies in far too many instances. Sure, there might have been a few things that were changed, but overall, attitudes, smaller laws, local laws, and the overall problems of society haven't been resolved.

We are often quick to assume the issues we had once upon a time we don't have anymore. It's easy to look around our lives and our social circles and pretend that the problems of the past aren't a part of our society anymore. We get so busy with our jobs, cars, families, households, and immediate life circumstances that we pretend having all these things are signs of advancements, that society isn't where it used to be anymore and won't return to its roots, when the unfortunate facts are all around us that things aren't right in a general sense right in front of our faces.

If we want to be people of justice, we need to be aware of the injustices surrounding us on a daily basis. All over the world, right in our own country, right in our own cities, and right in our own backyard, there is someone being mistreated due to outdated laws or social customs that make such mistreatment perfectly legal or socially acceptable. They are things so commonplace, most people don't think about them and those who are mistreated don't seek justice because they know they won't find a remedy readily available. Recognizing these things provides us with a mission field right in our own backyard, with plenty of people who are hurting or are hardened by an unjust society, who need to experience the loving touch of purpose and justice by those who can reiterate whatever they experience was, indeed, wrong.

Sometimes people need to know that other people are watching and aware of the wrong things that have happened to them in their lives. It takes a special person to do something about wrong, not just on a political or national level, but on the immediate level, reaching out to the one who hurts and showing them that there are people who wake up and pay attention, not ignoring nor forgetting the things that go on right in front of them. We may not all be people who can influence and change governmental powers, but we can certainly be people who influence and change the lives of those who feel the sting of injustice at work in their lives. We can also be people who recognize what is right in front of them and who work for right in our own lives, ensuring that we uphold principles of equality and truth, right where we are.

- DAILY DISCIPLINE: TAKE AN INTEREST IN AN INJUSTICE CASE; LEARN MORE ABOUT IT AND PROMOTE THE TRUTH THEREIN.

- Day 18 -
You Like it...but do You Share it?

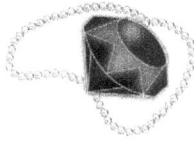

Do not forget [neglect] to do good to others,
and share with them, because such sacrifices please God.
(Hebrews 13:6)

- DAILY READING: ACTS 4:32-35

*S*ocial media is flooded with videos, pictures, links, news headlines and other sources of information found all over the internet. It's obvious from watching who shares what and how people share what they like where they get their information from and who they consider to be their relevant sources of information. What is most interesting is to watch different people pop up, like something posted, go on and on about how relevant they feel it is, how much they like it...and then leave it right there, on its page, because of the source where it came from.

Much of the time we ignore the truth that stares us in the face because we don't like where it came from. We've grown accustomed to the circles we are in and the facts we circulate so much that we dislike when something comes along (no matter how true it might be) from another source. If the "wrong side" said it, then we might like it...we might agree with it...but we will make sure we never, ever share it!

Alliances can be great things. It's important that we know how to work with other people and that we can put aside differences that don't mean much to edify someone or something else that is more important than just us. Alliances become a problem, however, when we are willing to forsake the truth about something because the message comes in a package we don't like or from a group that seems contradictory to our own values.

Many causes could be enhanced and furthered if we were willing to validate our own causes with information generated from different sources. One of the biggest killers of a cause is the inability to generate interest and information in that particular issue beyond a small circle of people who feel it is important. We have done this in many ways with our spiritual beliefs as well as those we hold dear to us from a social perspective, and doing so makes sure that whatever we want to get out there will be withheld because we are afraid our enemies might make it ahead of us if we promote informative statistics they provide.

We also do this with the businesses, causes, ministries, and work of our friends. We'll be the first ones to like and share a meme that has circulated around the internet millions of times, but what about sharing information about the businesses our friends own, the ministries and sermons our friends preach, the causes and organizations most dear to their hearts, or the works that our friends have created? Do you share their books, review them online, buy their make-up or other goods, or support their different products?

The causes we all have will be much more fruitful and productive if we share with one another and encourage one another through information, education, and products, no matter where they come from. In this, we will find a bigger sense of unity and purpose and can move to greater things.

- DAILY DISCIPLINE: TAKE SOME TIME AND REVIEW A BOOK OR PRODUCT ONLINE THAT YOU BOUGHT FROM A FRIEND.

- DAY 19 -
Proclaiming Freedom to the Captives

H<small>E</small> HAS SENT ME...TO TELL THE CAPTIVES THEY ARE FREE...
(I<small>SAIAH</small> 61:1)

- D<small>AILY</small> R<small>EADING</small>: E<small>XODUS</small> 6:1-13

When we were kids, one of the worst punishments was being "grounded." When we were grounded, we couldn't do anything outside of the house except go to school or church. We would spend our grounded days doing chores, homework, and sitting around the house very bored, at that, because being grounded meant we couldn't watch television, listen to the radio, or do anything fun. When we were grounded, we were supposed to think about whatever it was we did wrong and make a point not to do it again.

This is an example of what it means to be "captive" or bound in captivity on a level that most people have experienced. When the Bible speaks of "captives," however, it is speaking of far more than just being grounded by parents because someone did something wrong. In fact, such individuals often become captives through no fault of their own as captives start out living their lives and moving about via average circumstances, not expecting anything out of the ordinary to happen to them. A Biblical captive was someone identified as a prisoner of war, forcibly confined or restricted by a government or rebel power who came in and took over another city, region, or country. Being a captive meant being forced to subject oneself to another government, often confined, abused, beaten, or mistreated to the point of slavery as people were used for pawns and control among the ruling powers of the day.

Captives do exist in this literal sense, even today. While statistics are hard to come by, there is no question that prisoners of war and civilians go missing every day in various parts of the world due to war and rebel groups attempting to overthrow different governments and gain control. Captives are a primary way groups acquire control and bargaining power to get what they want, and in that unfortunate power play, people suffer, lose their livelihood and possessions, and in many instances, lose their lives.

To proclaim freedom to the captives means those who live as the pawns of unjust social politics are now free; those politics have dissipated, and they are able to live their lives in the open, without the limitations of controlled captivity. Being free meant a new day was to come, with the possibilities of a new life and new challenges to be lived. Freedom for someone who has been bound is not just the opposite of captivity; it is the answer to it.

There are many ways that people find themselves captive without politics or prisoners of war. We can be captive to our upbringings, to outdated ideas that make us ineffective witnesses of the Gospel, to our ideas or thinking, to abuse or mistreatment incurred at some point in our lives, to our pasts, or to our sinful states. No matter who someone is or what they have been through, they too need to embrace the message of freedom, recognizing that the anecdote to captivity is true freedom found in Christ.

- DAILY DISCIPLINE: LEARN ABOUT CURRENT FIGURES WHO STAND AS POLITICAL PRISONERS AND WRITE A LETTER ADVOCATING FOR THEIR FREEDOM.

- DAY 20 -
Becoming Good Role Models

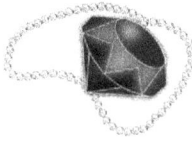

No, your beauty should come from within you [your inner self; the hidden/secret person of the heart]—the beauty of a gentle and quiet spirit that will never be destroyed [fade; perish] and is very precious [very valuable; of great worth] to God [Prov. 31:30].
(1 Peter 3:4)

- DAILY READING: EPHESIANS 5:1-20

One of my personal complaints about reality television is the way women are portrayed in such programs. We never see reality shows about women who are pursuing law, medicine, ministry, or business. What we see instead are women who are catty and uncontrolled, screaming, clawing, and backbiting one another in an unglorified manner, acting as if they have no civilized manners whatsoever within themselves. The women of reality television tend to be women who are notable for attitude rather than aptitude and many are on the shows they are on because they have married men with status or are good at frivolously spending money.

It disturbs me when I see young girls emulating the behavior they have seen prevalent in women of these programs. As much as adults watch these programs for questionable reasons, having our girls see these programs processes differently within their minds. Where adults might see the programming and say "What in the world..." young girls think these women are on television because they are doing something notable and important, and therefore, their behaviors should be emulated.

The result are little girls who behave more like divas than little girls, quick to demand and act out in behaviors that they see in women prevalent in these programs. While adults might think they are funny at first, they reveal a much deeper problem that relates to female image and what it means to be a woman within society.

I don't ascribe to the belief that being a woman means sitting around in pumps all day and wearing skirts and hats throughout our entire lives. I think that being a woman means being a woman, and being a woman takes several different adaptations depending on the woman. There is one thing, however, that we need to keep in mind when it comes to talking about being a good woman, and that is the principle of being a good role model. If we want our girls to emulate good values and become women who want to make the world around them a better place, we need to make sure we model those values to them. If all our girls see are us laughing at women on television who live a scripted reality, our girls are going to think that's what it takes to be famous and to be important or valued.

The question becomes, what are you doing as a woman to be a good role model to the girls and young women around you? Are you aware of how you speak, the causes you take on, the interests you have, the work you do, and the kind of worker you are? Are you aware that when you are at home or in a relationship with someone, the girls around you are watching? It is time for us to stop assuming that the engulfing nature of culture cannot be changed if we do the right thing. We can turn tides, and we can give our young girls the message they can be anything they want if they will work hard and make the effort…all if we are willing to be good role models for them by living what we tell them we want them to do.

- DAILY DISCIPLINE: MENTOR A YOUNG GIRL THAT YOU KNOW, BEING CONSCIOUS OF HOW YOU CARRY YOURSELF.

- DAY 21 -
The Social Call of the Prophet: Justice

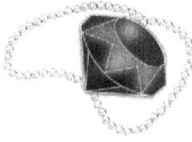

BEFORE THE LORD GOD DOES ANYTHING, HE TELLS HIS PLANS
TO HIS SERVANTS THE PROPHETS.
(AMOS 3:7)

• DAILY READING: AMOS 3:1-15

Contrary to popular understanding, the call of the prophet is not to spend their days sitting around in heavenly places, having vision after vision. Just like the rest of the Ephesians 4:11 ministry, the prophet has a social call, something God has invested within each prophet in order to help train the Body of Christ to handle different matters. In the case of the prophet, that social call is justice, or the principle of upholding fairness and equity within a societal understanding.

There is no way that we can study the work of the Old Testament prophets and not see the component of justice shine through their works. While we often teach their work was to convict of sin, most of the sins they spoke on were not things that people today would consider "big" sins. The prophets of old understood the connection between idolatry and adultery, murder, using money to intimidate or control the poor, stealing in the form of bribes or dishonesty, lying, inhospitality, blemished sacrifices and offerings, or withholding something from God. All these different things were social injustices, things that helped people retain power and control other people unjustly, and they were things the prophets of their day sought to correct so the nation or nations in question would not experience God's judgment.

In the case of Old Testament prophets, justice was an integral part of the law. Just like in our world today, people believed if they could find a loophole, it didn't mean they actually violated the law; it just meant that they were finding a way around the strict regulations contained therein. When it came to the prophets, there wasn't this loophole area where people's lives were at stake. Calling the injustices exactly what they were, the Old Testament prophets spent their lives challenging the comfortable establishment that didn't want to hear their loopholes were, in fact, a violation of God's principles.

A true prophet of God is not going to be someone who is so super-spiritual, they are untouchable in this world. They are, likewise, not going to be people who perpetrate injustice by using false prophecies of houses, money, and cars to steal the money of the poor and the hopeless so they can live a larger-than-life existence. True prophets care when anyone is killed by authority figures or by systems that are supposed to be set up to establish and enforce justice in the land. True prophets will speak up for what is true and just, even if the entire church of the day rejects them.

Prophets are people who speak for God, which means they need to be hearing from Him. It's tempting to absorb the common speech of the day that revolves around end-times panic, social comforts, or encouragements that don't manifest. A true prophet, however, will speak forth the words of justice that God gives them, in each and every situation, without social popularities or encouragements.

- DAILY DISCIPLINE: SPEAK OUT AGAINST INJUSTICES THAT YOU SEE.

- DAY 22 -

Developing Patience as We Wait for Change

BUT WE ARE HOPING FOR SOMETHING WE DO NOT HAVE YET,
AND WE ARE WAITING FOR IT PATIENTLY [WITH PERSEVERANCE].
(ROMANS 8:25)

- DAILY READING: ROMANS 5:1-8

When I was in my early twenties, I served as a lobbyist for women's issues before the New York State legislature. This is not nearly as glamorous as it sounds. It means I spent a lot of time reading up on current laws and issues. I also spent a few days per year at the capitol building in Albany, New York, visiting the offices of various lawmakers in our state to persuade them to vote in favor of our cause. What it amounted to is what I call a "lesson in futility." When one bill got passed, the victory was only temporary. Someone somewhere would discover a loophole that would make sure they didn't have to follow the newly passed laws and that would mean we would have to start all over again with a new bill that would answer the loophole found in the old one. It was a long process that didn't seem to have a formidable end anywhere in sight.

One of the major reasons I left politics and lobbying was because I never felt that change came from what I was doing. It felt like I was spending a lot of time trying to urge politicians to adapt laws that they couldn't relate to nor understand within their own life experience. The politicians sat behind desks and most of them had been in their respective positions for twenty years or more, not having much to do with real life or the real-life experiences of the women whose lives would be affected by the laws or the lack thereof.

The one thing I learned from my experiences in lobbying is that change doesn't come overnight. It might seem like the laws that are put into place within a nation just show up one day and knock on your door, but groups of people spend years working to make sure those laws came into being. The truth of change is that it doesn't just knock on our door and show up in our lives, but it is present there and works its way into our lives as the realities of change start to take over. As we wait for change to come forth, especially when it is hard, we have to develop the needed fruit of patience.

Patience isn't something we like to hear about in general, let alone when we are dealing with circumstances that relate to injustice, wrongdoing, or general societal issues that we want to see change. We don't like the idea that wrongdoing seems to pervade or "win" for a season, and it can cause us to feel frustrated and aggravated by our process. Patience reminds us, however, that change comes with the heart of each person we touch, each mind we reach, and that if we are willing to be patient and move through the process, the change we seek will eventually come.

Patience doesn't mean sitting around, waiting, hoping things will get better on their own. Patience is continued persistence, the purpose, the pursuit of what is right even when we don't see the results we desire to see right away. Patience is an active, not passive, position. It takes every step we see and every fulfillment of each step as a positive sign, one that reminds us of the dawn ahead if we keep working.

- DAILY DISCIPLINE: PICK UP A PROJECT OR ASSIGNMENT YOU LET GO BECAUSE YOU GREW IMPATIENT WITH ITS PROCESS.

- DAY 23 -
I Was a Stranger, and You Invited Me in

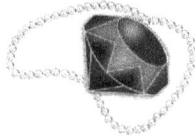

...I WAS ALONE AND AWAY FROM HOME [A STRANGER], AND YOU INVITED ME
INTO YOUR HOUSE [WELCOMED/RECEIVED ME].
(MATTHEW 25:35)

- DAILY READING: HEBREWS 13:1-3

*H*omelessness is one of those issues we hear about on the news, feel bad about for a few minutes, and then go about our regularly scheduled programming without another thought as pertains to the people featured on that news segment. The realities about homelessness are a lot closer than someone in another state or other country, and they cause disruption to more than just having a home to come home to at night. Homelessness leads to hunger, disruptions in childhood education, lack of resources, and an inability to hold down a job and keep families together. As challenging as it is to run a household under normal conditions, imagine how much more complicated – and unpleasant – it is to try and maintain such when the comforts of home no longer exist.

There are approximately 3.5 million homeless people in the United States, with approximately 1.35 million of that population consisting of children.[5] In any given city on any night, most homeless shelters are at capacity, forcing them to turn away people in need of a bed for the night. Despite what we might want to hope, homelessness is also on the increase, especially due to post-recession recoveries that have not yet happened. Coming back from a homeless experience, coupled with many of the side effects of homelessness, which can include loss of family and friends, having to relocate, domestic violence, or substance abuse, homelessness is a serious and widespread problem that is not easily solved if we change the channel when a report about it comes on our television screens.

The answer to combat homelessness is to use proper wisdom in the promise of hospitality that can be extended to those in need, whether we know them personally, or not. Whether or not we want to hear it, God commands us to be hospitable to other people. Hospitality is more than coffee and donuts after church service. The essence and heart of hospitality is willing to be of service to others in a manner that extends beyond just meeting a surface need. If we want to be people who invite strangers, that starts with the atmosphere we set in our churches and ministries. It requires us to know the proper avenues to help those who are facing homelessness and, if they don't exist in your area, then it should be of primary concern to see that something exists or is started to help the problem. It's not practical to suggest that every homeless person you meet can stay in your house, but it is practical to look at the problem of homelessness and realize opening the doors of a church or ministry for the homeless can be a way to invite strangers and help a serious problem at the same time.

Every one of us can be personally hospitable to family or friends who fall on hard times. Whether it is letting someone stay with you, offering them a meal or some groceries, helping someone to find a job, or helping someone to find new housing, there are plenty of ways that you can help others who are down on their luck.

- DAILY DISCIPLINE: HAVE SOMEONE OVER TO YOUR HOME WHO YOU KNOW IS IN NEED.

- DAY 24 -
Do the Work That Someone Else Doesn't Want to do

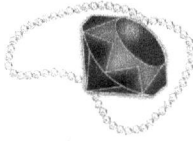

JESUS SAID TO HIS FOLLOWERS [DISCIPLES], "THERE ARE MANY PEOPLE TO
HARVEST [THE HARVEST IS GREAT/LARGE] BUT THERE ARE ONLY A FEW
WORKERS [THE WORKERS/LABORERS ARE FEW].
(MATTHEW 9:37)

- DAILY READING: MATTHEW 22:1-14

I was dealing with a trying and difficult season of ministry when
I read the Biblical parable of the wedding feast and suddenly
heard the excuses so many use to avoid being truly committed
to ministry today. Examining that passage made me realize the excuses
people use to avoid involvement – too busy at home, got married, got a
husband/wife to take care of, have children, busy at work, busy with
life, uninterested to celebrate someone else or do something for
someone else – are not new. In fact, they are apparently as old as time
itself, because we find them to be excuses people would have heard in
the first century as well as the twenty-first.

When it comes to the work of change, there are many people who
will line up to attend a black-tie banquet once a cause is popular and all
the celebrities endorse it. The problem with this approach to social
activism is most causes don't reach this point easily, and many fall from
popularity as quickly as they reach celebrity status. While people wait
for cocktail fundraisers and fancy billionaire investors, people who are
the most in need go without, go invisible, and hurt, time and time again,
because nobody wants to take an interest in meeting their needs right
now.

If we mean what we say when we claim to want change, we need
to pay careful attention to our excuses for not doing something and for
not getting involved. If we are constantly blaming family, friends, work,
home, life in general for not getting involved, we are missing the entire
point of what life is supposed to be about. If we don't get involved
because a cause doesn't seem prestigious enough, it would do us good

to look at ourselves in a deeper way and ask why. The problems of this world do not wrap themselves up in comfortable, easy ideals that are fun to handle, good for show, and don't cost us anything in our lives. If we want to make change, we need to take the time from our lives, encourage our families to come along and roll up their sleeves as well, be good role models, and make the difference for someone else who can't easily or ever pay us back because that is who we are called to be.

Be the change you want to see in the world. We've seen it on memes and bumper stickers, and we've echoed it in our heads and our minds when it comes to new challenges or complicated things. It's no different here when it comes to change and to being willing to roll up our sleeves and do something that's not easy, prestigious, or cute to do simply because it needs doing and we are here to do just that.

The needed changes present in this world can't wait until a cause is infamous. They can't wait until it is a convenient time in your life, when it seems like no one else needs you or demands your time and attention. If you want to be someone who changes the world, start by setting your sights on doing things that others don't feel are important enough to do.

- DAILY DISCIPLINE: START WORK ON A PROJECT THAT ADDRESSES INJUSTICES AT A GRASSROOTS LEVEL.

- Day 25 -

Blessed are the Meek

They are blessed who are humble [meek; gentle], for the whole earth
will be theirs [they shall inherit the earth; Ps. 37:11].
(Matthew 5:5)

- Daily Reading: Psalm 25:8-22

As I write this devotional, it is a presidential election year in the United States. To say it has been an interesting process to watch is an understatement. The candidates for president on all sides, from all parties, have spent the past several months trying to display their intense abilities to control and dominate the process. There have been open public fights, mudslinging, and arguments as one candidate tries to discredit the other. There have even been intense fights among people of the same party prior to the convention nominations! With the whole world watching, the entire process has been embarrassing and disgraceful, to say the least.

The one quality I have not yet seen is meekness, or a willingness to show a quiet and gentle nature that avoids deliberate quarreling and fighting. If anything, being argumentative appears to be a pattern of behavior exhibiting prowess, control, and a take-charge attitude. What is most disturbing to me are the vast numbers of proclaimed Christians who seem to think these unhumble, argumentative attitudes are properly ordained for leadership within this nation by their proclaimed personal revelations.

God has told us those who are meek are blessed, because they will inherit, or receive, the earth. This might not sound like much to us, especially when we want to bring forth change by force because it's not coming quickly enough, but it is a great purpose and divine promise. It proves to us that change by force or violence is never the answer, because force and violence will lead to more force and violence as people get caught up in the moment and fail to remember what they are fighting for in the first place. Rather, as people of God, our best show of integrity and belief in our own cause is to operate as peaceful people, not self-seeking, and to walk our prescribed course, because in the end, the inheritance of the earth and the authority that comes forth with that promise shall belong to us.

It might seem like people who advocate force or violence get their way all the time, but such amounts to bullying that catches up with them as unpopular leaders and founders of highly criticized and questionable movements. Force equates to antics which equate to attention, but true meekness, which can endure and transcend generations, comes to those who are willing to behave properly, present their viewpoints with grace and dignity, and refrain from forcing other people to follow or embrace the viewpoints that one espouses. Yes, of course, we know that you believe in your cause, but there is someone else, somewhere, who does not believe in it…and the sooner you can accept that viewpoint, the easier meekness will become.

Meek people are not weak. If anything, they are the embodiment of strength under pressure, challenge in the face of change, and purpose in the face of all good things that come to those who are willing to walk out change for the duration.

- DAILY DISCIPLINE: GET OFF YOUR HIGH PEDESTAL AND HUMBLE YOURSELF!

- DAY 26 -
Remember that God is Good

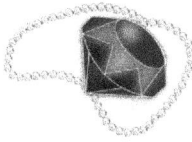

EVERY GOOD ACTION [OR ACT OF GIVING] AND EVERY PERFECT GIFT IS FROM
GOD [COMES FROM ABOVE]. THESE GOOD GIFTS COME DOWN FROM THE
CREATOR OF THE SUN, MOON, AND STARS [THE FATHER OF LIGHTS;
REFERRING TO GOD'S CREATION OF THE HEAVENLY BODIES (GEN. 1:14–19;
PS. 136:7–9; JER. 31:35)], WHO DOES NOT CHANGE LIKE THEIR SHIFTING
SHADOWS.
(JAMES 1:17)

- DAILY READING: LAMENTATIONS 3:19-33

*I*njustice. Crime. Poverty. Homelessness. Racism. Sexism. Discrimination. Substance abuse. If we look around our world, it's easy to conclude that the entire world is hopeless. I have met many activists, ministers, and others alike who got to a point where they couldn't stand any more despair, heartache, hurt or the pains they saw and decided there was nothing more they could do, so they started retreating to a dark place. Many concluded God didn't exist or if He did exist, He didn't care at all about humankind or what they were going through.

It pains me to see this happen to the best of warriors who are most committed to change and making great things happen in the world. At the same time, I understand the reason those who are most involved often become the most disillusioned. When it seems like the cause is greater than the help and that one starts to drown in helping rather than seeing progress, it's easy to fall into a place of despair and wonder where all the help is that is supposed to step up and assist in the things that God has commanded us to do.

It's not God's failure that we lack proper help for the different causes out there, nor is it God's failure that those causes exist. It's our failure, our sinful state, our inhumanity to others, and our lack of motivation to do anything about the things that surround us every day that are wrong. Yes, we might take interest in one cause, but there are many, many more around us we don't take interest in, or we are unable to support because there is only one of us. The reality is, however, that if we all took on one or two, particularly causes that don't get a lot of attention or notoriety, there would be plenty of us working to bring forth hope and help and it would help alleviate some of the problems that do exist.

Despite the things we see around us…even though there are not enough laborers in the harvest…God is still with us and God is still good. He takes the little bit that we have, and we can offer and turns it into something that blesses more lives than just those of our immediate selves. God still loves us, He is still with us, and He still guides us through the difficulties and trials we encounter as we try to help others.

There's nothing wrong with getting tired every now and then and needing a break. The best of warriors needs a break every now and then to let someone else take over the stress and difficulty of constant battle. Getting tired doesn't mean you need to quit and give up on your faith and everything else that goes along with that. It means you take a break; you refresh and renew yourself, and allow God to pour into you, speaking truth and filling your senses with His presence so you remember why you do what you do while you are doing it. When you are ready to get back up, you start again, realizing in all things just how good God is because you are a part of His plan to change the world and bless other people.

- DAILY DISCIPLINE: DON'T GIVE UP!

- Day 27 -
Adopted as Children of God

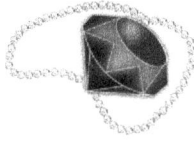

Because of His love [this phrase may go with the previous sentence], God had already decided to make us His own children [predestined us for adoption] through Jesus Christ. That was what He wanted and what pleased Him.
(Ephesians 1:5)

- Daily Reading: Romans 8:14-19

Not unlike today, people in Biblical times placed a great deal of emphasis on having their own children. Families were a part of kinship and inheritance, which transferred between fathers and sons. If a girl married a man and she had no brothers, her family's property would become that of her husband's family, causing property transference and sometimes poverty for living relatives. The burden to produce a male heir fell with the female, as people back then did not understand biology and the role that men play in determining the sex of offspring. That means women who were unable to produce a male heir were deemed as inferior, sometimes divorced or abandoned by their husbands, and seen as a problem within their marriage. Let it not be lost on anyone that this was all due to cultural demands and pressures, and it all boiled down to property and money.

Adoption, therefore, was not something that was seen as a first, or preferential choice. It was part of Greek culture, but not a big part of Jewish culture. In fact, adoption wasn't regarded in the same way as we do today. Infant adoption was rare. Most of the time, older children were brought to live with other families as slaves and sometimes a householder would raise one of the children as a son or daughter. The rights extended to these children were sometimes a little different than we understand adoption today, but in a larger sense, the principle of adoption became the same: someone who was not related by birth became a part of a household because they did not have blood relatives who were able or willing to take care of them.

Today medical technology has created many resources to try and aid parents in biological conception whereas it would have at one time been impossible. This means extensive money and resources are spent trying to conceive a biological child rather than investigating into adoption or giving a home to children who don't have one. While I can certainly understand many people want their own children, there is also something to be said for the work of adoption and for creating families from adoption, as well.

I once heard that if only three percent of all professing Christians in the world would adopt one child, there would be no children left for adoption anywhere in the world. As believers who embrace a higher spiritual reality than those that relate to worldly lineages, adoption is a spiritual principle, one that we should all thank God for. You see, every one of us came into this world via biology, but thanks to God, we are all now a part of His family, a part of something that never ends. One day, our family lineages will die out; it is just something that happens as a part of nature. Because of God, our spiritual family will live, forever and ever, into eternity. Adoption is something to consider for any open and willing family because it lives this very principle in one's own family life. By adopting a child with no family, they become a part of yours and experience their own living type of the Kingdom of God.

- DAILY DISCIPLINE: EITHER LOOK INTO ADOPTION FOR YOUR OWN FAMILY OR SUPPORT A FAMILY WHO HAS ADOPTED A CHILD OR IS IN THE PROCESS OF DOING SO.

- DAY 28 -
The Blessing of Anger

When you are angry [are disturbed; tremble], do not sin.
Think about these things [Meditate; Speak to your heart] quietly
as you go to bed [on your bed]. Selah [Interlude]
(Psalm 4:4)

- Daily Reading: Matthew 21:12-17

I don't hear it as much now, but in the mid-2000s, one of the biggest things labeled as a sin was "anger." People used to talk about anger as being a sin and being something we needed to erase from our lives all together. It used to concern me when I would hear this because it was another one of those examples of people taking something in the Bible out of context, turning it into something else, but doing so with the vibe that the statement sounded holy and altruistic. Surely being angry does sound like a bad thing to our ears, right? It would be much better if we could avoid all anger and try to be people who are happy and smiling all the time...right?

Wrong! This serious misconception makes it sound like Christians should be people who walk around all day, with a half-grin because we wouldn't want to smile too much, as if we are living our lives on a tranquilizer. Does this sound like the way that God desires us to live our lives? If we recognize our experience with God and with others to be relationship-based, that means they are relationships. Relationships come with good, bad, and everything in the middle, and that God – and those who we are in relationship with – must come to a place where they can handle our different emotions and feelings, whether they are good, bad, or indifferent. It's fine to teach and expound upon ways to recognize anger that is selfish or self-centered in nature, but it is not fine to teach anger is a sin. Like all things God has given to us, anger has its place, and it's important to learn the difference between throwing a tantrum and being genuinely upset when something around you is not right.

There is such a thing as righteous anger. When Jesus threw the money changers out of the temple, He did so because He was angry. Someone once pointed out to me that He didn't turn the tables over in the temple to get some good exercise. That same righteous anger lives in all of us as believers, who stand back in fury and alarm when things around them and things in this world are simply not right. Anger stands as our spiritual alarm clock, ready to go off and alert us to something that needs change, and the force of anger exists to motivate us to do something about whatever it is that's not right.

Anger exists to stir us up to good works, not to move us to abuse others or damage property. It does not exist to post angry, ranting words online, as none of these things will bring about clear or lasting change. Anger is a boundary line set within us, and it is a blessing that we should never ignore nor take for granted. God has seen to it in many ways that we will be people motivated to act and do things to change our world for the better, and anger is one of those motivating factors that cause us to rise up, dust ourselves off, and start doing something to bring about the world we desire to see.

- DAILY DISCIPLINE: EXAMINE YOUR ANGER AND USE IT TO IGNITE CHANGE.

- DAY 29 -

Communion is More than Just Bread and Wine

- DAILY READING: 1 CORINTHIANS 10:1-22

Different churches believe different things surrounding the doctrine of communion. I grew up in a church that taught Jesus was literally present in the bread and wine of communion and when we took communion, we were literally taking in His flesh and blood. It sounds strange to most when I talk about that with others, but the truth is we all have different communion traditions that have popped up over the centuries. They all might sound just as strange to someone else. For example, I was preaching in a church many years ago that had a communion table up front. I put my Bible down on it, not realizing that doing so was considered very taboo. I've been present in many churches that require the ushers to dress in a certain attire and do not allow those who distribute communion to touch the elements without wearing gloves. Some churches require the entire congregation to come dressed in a certain color or style of dress. Others make elaborate rules as to who can receive communion and who cannot, all done under the auspices of the church.

To us as Christians, communion is a ceremony. It is something we do in memory of Jesus Christ's death for us, and it is something we shall do in memory of His death until He returns. Communion, however, is symbolic of more than just a ceremony or of the meal that Christ shared with His disciples before He died. Communion represents a unity, a coming together because all have the shared experience of acknowledging Christ as our Savior and being raised to new life in Him. Communion is a symbol not just of our union with God, but our union with other believers, as well. It shows we have a common spiritual formation and one Savior, and we are here together in one Lord, one body, one Spirit, one faith, one baptism, one hope, and one God and Father of all.

In a book on activism, why is the concept of communion important? Because we, as Christians, need to remember the relevance of unity and the foundations of unity in our own lives and our work. Those foundations of unity give us the ability to focus on what is truly important and let go of the things that are not when it comes to our walk of faith with other believers. In the Kingdom, we are not going to like everybody. All of us are at different points in our journey of faith and all of us are at different levels of belief and understanding. Many of us come with baggage unique to our upbringing and from the different denominations we've belonged to throughout the years. Communion reminds us these things don't matter as long as we are in spiritual process, moving toward deeper things and away from the things that cause us to break faith and avoid the unity present in our faith community.

In communion, we learn about true unity. In learning about true unity, we learn how to connect to other people for any purpose and what to pick up and what to put aside. Simply put, we learn how to be a part of a cause greater than ourselves.

- DAILY DISCIPLINE: HAVE A COMMUNION SERVICE WITH YOUR WOMEN'S GROUP, A FEW FRIENDS, OR YOUR FAMILY.

- DAY 30 -
Releasing Prisoners from Darkness

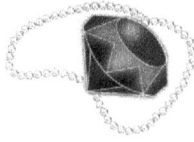

He has sent me...to tell the prisoners they are released.
(Isaiah 61:1)

- DAILY READING: PSALM 69:30-36

*I*n the various states I've lived in, I have always made a point to be involved in some way with the prisons present there. A lost and often forgotten aspect of ministry work, prison ministry is a difficult work that takes a lot of discernment, a lot of heart, and a very keen ability to read people and situations. If you've ever been to a prison, you know what I am talking about. The coldness of the environment, the protests of prisoners, the abuses we know go on (on both sides of population and administration) and the endless rules and corporal encounters call for the ability to understand, to listen, and to cover all offenses with love.

In New Testament times, prison conditions were beyond horrible. Even from earlier times, it was not uncommon for prisoners to be kept in dark, unsanitary conditions. Prisons were typically underground, tight, with small cells and narrow passageways. Prisoners often were sold as slaves or used within the Roman workforce, both within the government and the military.[6] Prison was associated with people of all backgrounds, not all of whom we would define as criminals today. Inmates could be those who broke laws, but were also those who were prisoners of war, captives, sometimes those who didn't have families, vagrants, or the very, very poor who were unable to pay back debts. There were also those arrested who broke laws as pertaining to religious or cultural codes, things that we would never imagine people to be arrested for in our lifetimes. The apostles and early disciples who were arrested for preaching and proclaiming Christ were arrested on charges such as this, because their words threatened the religious beliefs of the day that were deeply saturated into their local cultures.

The concept of releasing prisoners from darkness is, therefore, more than just a commentary on the darkness of the prison lifestyle, although that can certainly apply in the context of the passage. Prisoners in ancient times (and most likely in many cultures around the world today as well) were used to living in dark conditions where they did not comfortably see the light of day. To take a prisoner out of darkness meant to release them from prison, to bring them to a place of freedom.

It's easy for us to sit back and judge inmates based on the things they have been charged with. They may even be things they admit they did earlier in time. We should also keep in mind that not everyone who goes to jail is guilty of a crime, and more often than not, there are those who have never been imprisoned who are guilty of crimes. More than this, releasing prisoners from where they are into a place of freedom indicates a position of forgiveness, of no longer requiring them to pay for something that they did that cannot now be undone. If God does this for us, as we are all guilty before Him of sin, then we should be that much more willing to stand back and release those in darkness so they too can taste the truth of freedom.

- DAILY DISCIPLINE: FIND AN INMATE PEN-PAL PROGRAM AND WRITE LETTERS OF ENCOURAGEMENT TO AN INMATE.

- DAY 31 -
Learning from History

THE THINGS THAT HAPPENED TO THOSE PEOPLE ARE EXAMPLES.
THEY WERE WRITTEN DOWN TO TEACH [INSTRUCT; WARN] US WHO LIVE
IN THE FINAL DAYS OF THIS AGE [FOR WHOM THE END/CLIMAX/CULMINATION
OF THE AGES HAS COME].
(1 CORINTHIANS 10:11)

- DAILY READING: DEUTERONOMY 4:9-14

I can recall not even a handful of students who were interested in history when I was in school. The way it was taught was exceedingly dry and it left out many interesting facts that pertain to history that might have made us more interested in the process. It didn't help that history teachers were notoriously boring and made the subject seem less interesting and applicable than it already did.

The major flaw with the way history is taught to children and young adults is simple: it isn't approached in a manner that seems to give us any insights or relevance to the world in which we live right now. It seems simple enough to say if those things that happened back then hadn't happened, we wouldn't be here now, but when we don't see the connection between history and right now, it doesn't seem that if those things had never happened, it would have much to do with us, right now, anyway.

When history is approached in college, however, the way it is taught is radically different from the way it is taught when we were younger. Missing details are filled in, information that was altered or taught improperly is corrected, and there is a greater emphasis in seeing us in historical events as we are right now rather than as distant events with no correlation to the present.

As kids we used to hear our elders say things like, "History repeats itself." The truth is that it does, but we can't recognize how it repeats itself if we have no connection to our history and that of our ancestors. We must discipline ourselves to study our past, our histories, the places where we have come from, so we can see the ways history repeats itself in our day. Historically speaking, our ancestors went through certain things and reaped the results of those things as they either ignored them or tried to handle them in some fashion. Reading about their results: good, bad, and indifferent are what give us the edge to handle things today instead of aimlessly trying to change things by making the same mistakes of the past.

In many churches today we are told to forget our past and our histories, acting as if they never happened. It's treated as if it is kind of there, but we don't embrace it, accept it as our own, and treat it as if it has any part of us right now, because it is seen as too messy, too unimportant, not what we should want to entertain. This approach sounds too much like the watered-down histories we were not inclined to receive as kids. In true spiritual fashion, we are called to learn from our pasts, our mistakes, and our histories, rejoicing in the realities that we have a rich history to learn from that consist both of victories and defeats, things to embrace and things to reject, and overall, things that challenge us as believers and call us to places of change.

Learn from history. Embrace history as a part of who you are as a person, one who has your own unique stamp to place on the history of your life and the lineage of history itself.

- DAILY DISCIPLINE: GIVE YOUR TESTIMONY.

- DAY 32 -
Pray for Our Leaders

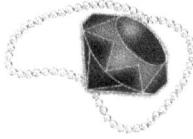

PRAY FOR RULERS [KINGS] AND FOR ALL WHO HAVE AUTHORITY SO THAT
WE CAN HAVE QUIET AND PEACEFUL LIVES FULL OF WORSHIP AND RESPECT
FOR GOD [IN ALL GODLINESS AND DIGNITY/REVERENCE].
(1 TIMOTHY 2:2)

- DAILY READING: 1 TIMOTHY 2:1-8

*I*t's very common to see different posts online either for or against certain leaders we have in office today. It would appear from first glance that most people have very strong feelings about the leadership of their nation. Some are very in favor of a leader while others are very opposed to that leadership, for one reason or another. It's obvious from watching the varied opinions that we do not agree, as people, on what is best for our cities, towns, states, provinces, and countries. We all feel the best answer to get from where we are to where we want to be is based upon the opinions we have formed, and the opinions we have formed are, most likely, based on the information we have received on a specific issue.

The problem with this theory is that the information we receive isn't always accurate. If anything, much of the information we receive is tainted based on the opinions of the news outlets or broadcasters who do the research. Somewhere in all the information we receive, the truth can be found, although it is not always obvious where it lies on the surface. Littered with opinions, the sways of thought, and the hopes the information provided will prove a viewpoint rather than the truth, getting to the bottom of information as is presented on political and social issues through the media is often a job all its own.

In the midst of our host of opinions about leadership, how many of us can honestly say we stop and pray for our leaders? If you are a leader of a ministry or a leader in any capacity, you can testify to how difficult leadership is. It seems as if things never go right all the time and that it's impossible to keep everyone happy all the time. The feelings of inadequacy, self-doubt, frustration, and difficulty, especially in trial, can easily wear a leader out. With many tasks, little help, and great work to do, leadership is something that is not easy, nor is it easily managed.

The reality is that most leaders reading this book probably don't have ministries, organizations, businesses, or tasks to do that involve the population of an entire nation or even region. Most of us don't have to turn on the internet, day after day, to find headlines, satires, blogs, or opinions about the different things we are doing or the jobs we are doing. We don't have to see political cartoons drawn about us and the mistakes we make. We're ready to run and hide because of the opinions of one or two people that quickly fade when they have someone else to talk about, but we are critical of leaders who must face these criticisms and pressures, day after day, and still put on a brave face to handle the needs and duties that their jobs require.

Being a leader is not easy. Being leaders over many people and over many different types of people is very hard, and that means whether you love a leader, or you want them out of office, they need prayer to do their jobs well and to do things properly. Next time, instead of criticizing an official, pray for them instead.

- DAILY DISCIPLINE: PRAY FOR THE LEADERS OF YOUR NATION AS WELL AS THE LEADERS OF ALL NATIONS.

- DAY 33 -
The Social Call of the Evangelist: Mercy

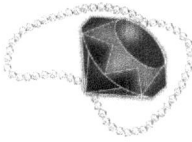

SO YOU MUST SHOW MERCY TO OTHERS, OR GOD WILL NOT SHOW MERCY
TO YOU WHEN HE JUDGES YOU [FOR JUDGMENT IS WITHOUT MERCY TO THE
ONE WHO DOES NOT ACT MERCIFULLY]. BUT THE PERSON WHO SHOWS MERCY
CAN STAND WITHOUT FEAR AT THE JUDGMENT [BUT MERCY TRIUMPHS OVER
JUDGMENT].
(JAMES 2:13)

- DAILY READING: TITUS 3:1-7

When I was a kid, we played a game called "mercy." One person would twist the arm or finger of the other person until that one would cry out "mercy" and then they were supposed to stop. It wasn't the nicest game we used to play, but it was common for a while, especially when I was around junior high age. It was one of those trends that came and went, and you would always know when it came back because you'd be waiting for the bus or on the schoolyard and all of a sudden, the phrase, "Mercy, mercy, MERCY!" would cry out of some kid's mouth who'd had enough of the revival of this little game we liked to play from time to time.

As odd as it might sound, the game (as vindictive as it might have been) did teach about the principle of mercy in a roundabout way. When playing that game, we would give someone else permission to mistreat or harm us in a certain way. When we asked for mercy, they would stop, even though they technically did not have to do so. We would cry for mercy and the other one would stop and release their hold on us. As quickly as we gave them power over us, they would relinquish power and set us free.

Mercy is a little word with a lot of power that doesn't seem to jolt us into spiritual consciousness like it should. It's a word we talk about from time to time and sing about often in songs, but I don't think we see its relevance in terms of our own lives or as people who believe in the social call of the Christian. We see this social call manifested in the work of the evangelist, who is called to make Christ real and present to those with whom they share the good news of the Gospel. Jesus Christ, in His very nature, was mercy-filled. He recognized that even though God had every right to execute judgment on humanity, that judgment would befall on Christ through His sacrifice. By making that ultimate sacrifice, mercy is ours: our sins might demand we are punished to the utmost degree of the law, but through Christ, the unrelenting punishment is no longer ours to receive.

As people who have received mercy, it is our position to live mercifully, as well. This means we must see mercy in our evangelists, in those who are called to model this for us: reflecting a caring heart, one that does not desire to see anyone perish, but hopes that people shall receive the Gospel and turn from their sins. In a social context, the work of mercy extends that understanding and kindness to others, no matter who they are, no matter what they are going through.

In mercy, we are all called to bless other people through the gift of understanding. No matter how hard or easy someone's life may appear to be, we are all going through something and dealing with the challenges of temptation and wrongdoing that cause us to call out and ask for mercy. If we want to be a people that truly reflect the heart of God, we will follow the example of the evangelist and walk in mercy.

- DAILY DISCIPLINE: SHOW MERCY IN A SITUATION WHERE YOU WOULD RATHER EXPRESS JUDGMENT.

- DAY 34 -
I Will not Be Silent

LORD, YOU HAVE BEEN WATCHING. DO NOT KEEP QUIET.
LORD, DO NOT LEAVE ME ALONE [BE FAR FROM ME].
(PSALM 35:22)

- DAILY READING: 2 SAMUEL 13:1-22

The season three, 23rd episode of the hit show *All In The Family* was titled "Gloria the Victim." In it, the character Gloria was walking home past a construction site and becomes the victim of attempted sexual assault. The episode accurately displays the conflict the family felt over whether to report the assault because of the way in which the court system and society would try and turn what happened to Gloria around to set the assailant free and victimize her all over again. The program introduced a concept, now known and discussed in many circles, as "rape culture" to the American public. By seeing the program and its effects on a beloved television character, it accurately showed how not only rape, but what happens afterward causes so many victims to remain silent.

The term "rape culture" is one that relates to the understanding that social teachings and practices about gender encourage rape and sexual assault in one form or another as a pervasive understanding within society. If we understand rape to be something is not about sex but is about using sex to exert power, rape culture is something that gives the inherent message that men are more powerful than women and rape is an unfortunate thing that happens because of something a woman did or didn't do. If we think about the way rape is treated in society, it is a very good example of the way victims are victimized all over again when they are told what happened to them is their fault. Women are blamed for rape in a variety of ways: their skirt was too short, it happened because of how they were dressed, they "asked" for it, they were drunk or high at the time, they willingly went out on a date with that individual, or they are accused of being an instigator in the whole process. Through rape culture, men are given the message they have no control over their behavior, women are responsible for male actions, and women who are raped should shut up because what was done to them was somehow deserved.

There is no such thing as consensual rape. There is such a thing, however, as rape jokes, which are defended by people, as street harassment and sexual harassment, where women do not feel safe on the streets at night or fear losing their jobs, and there is the very real facet that women who report rape often feel they are not taken seriously. The violation of rape is something so personal and that warrants so much judgment on the part of society and others that drives women into a place where they do not feel like they can talk about what happened to them because someone else will make sure to silence their voices.

Rape culture is a very real thing, just like rape and sexual assault. It happens to women of all ages, in all walks of life, and in all different situations. No woman deserves to have her voice silenced because someone else has already decided about what happened to her. When it comes to rape and sexual assault, we need to let our voices be heard, and step back and say, once and for all, I will not be silent.

- DAILY DISCIPLINE: SPEAK UP WHEN YOU ENCOUNTER EXAMPLES OF RAPE CULTURE, SUCH AS SOCIAL JOKES OR COMMENTARY.

- DAY 35 -
Positioned for Purpose

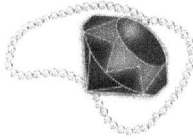

"COME AND SEE A MAN WHO TOLD ME EVERYTHING I EVER DID. DO YOU THINK HE MIGHT BE THE CHRIST [MESSIAH]?"
(JOHN 4:29)

- DAILY READING: JOHN 4:1-42

*G*rowing up in church I thought I knew about the woman at the well in John chapter 4. After all, she was a major figure in the Gospel of John. I'd heard preaching on her all my life, often spoken of in various forms of passing, although much of it was not particularly favorable. The male preachers I grew up hearing were quick to label her as a woman of poor reputation, even leveling her as a prostitute or worse, because the Bible says she lived with a man to whom she wasn't married. For the sake of argument, I will add the Bible does not state what kind of living arrangement she had; it only identifies the individual she lived with as being male. She could have been living with the man as his caretaker, with a male relative, with a family in preparation for marriage (as an engagement arrangement), or even platonically with a friend. It does not indicate they were living together and not married, as many indicate, reading the passage, today. What we don't often see in this woman, however, is that she was someone who was "positioned for purpose," there for a destiny to accomplish something for a purpose greater than herself.

Photini (history's name for this woman) was by all rights an apostle in the first century of Christianity. She was first credited with bringing her entire family to the Lord, including her five sisters and her son, and then spending the rest of her life in the work of the church. As a result of her singular ministry, many people were brought to the Lord. She was also the first apostle to the Gentiles, working among those who were not Jewish long before the Apostle Paul (or any of the others, for that matter) ever considered ministry or apostleship!

The woman at the well did some amazing work for the Lord and given her unique circumstances (whatever they might have been), God set her up to do that work, positioning her for that purpose, seeing through to something better than what existed at that moment in time. Sometimes we find ourselves in life circumstances that might, at least on the surface, seem like they open us up to the judgment of the world. God might ask us to be somewhere or do something that might not "sound right" according to church tradition or to the ears of those who have been told what sounds like God and what does not. We might have to deal with people who think they know everything about our situation, just like preachers do when it comes to Photini and her life. What we have to be careful to pay attention to, however, amidst the protests, the cries, and the questions as to why God has put us here, is our careful positioning and see what exactly God seeks to set up through our situation.

Having a Photini experience might not feel really good at that moment. It might feel like one is scrutinized, judged, and visibly out of sync with everyone else. The result, however, is the position raises above the situation, and the purpose shines through brighter than any circumstance one might have found themselves in prior.

- DAILY DISCIPLINE: EXAMINE WHERE YOU ARE AND USE THAT INFLUENCE TO DO SOMETHING USEFUL.

- DAY 36 -
Women in Ministry

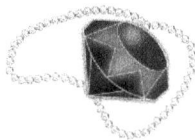

AND I ASK YOU, MY FAITHFUL [TRUE; GENUINE] FRIEND [COMPANION; YOKE-PARTNER; POSSIBLY A PROPER NAME: SYZYGOS], TO HELP THESE WOMEN. THEY SERVED [STRUGGLED; LABORED] WITH ME IN TELLING THE GOOD NEWS [GOSPEL], TOGETHER WITH CLEMENT AND OTHERS WHO WORKED WITH ME [THE REST OF MY COWORKERS], WHOSE NAMES ARE WRITTEN IN THE BOOK OF LIFE [REV. 3:5; 21:27].
(PHILIPPIANS 4:3)

- DAILY READING: ROMANS 16:1-6

Even though it might seem commonplace today, being a woman in ministry both is right now and has been for centuries a very revolutionary act. We were reminded of this when in the wake of civil and racial unrest two female pastors in South Carolina were threatened with attacks for no other reason than they were female and in ministry. It may be the twenty-first century, but a quick survey around many churches proves the issue of women in ministry has not resolved itself positively. Only 12% of congregations in the United States have a woman as their senior or solely ordained leader.[7] Some denominations show a percentage as low as 1% and others still show their percentages at zero, because they still refuse to ordain women. There are also seminaries that do not take a proactive stance on women in ministry and, as a result, either train or encourage women to take subordinate positions or work in churches as volunteers rather than pulpit ministers because of their own personal beliefs and values.

I don't think women who are not in active ministry understand the difficulty female ministers experience, often on a regular basis. Female ministers receive smaller offerings than their male counterparts and often find fewer opportunities to preach the Gospel because even churches that believe in women preachers often do so with conditions and give preferential positions and preaching opportunities to men.

Women who are in ministry still deal with stigma, opposition, lack of support and help, and constant innuendos they are not able to operate ministry and home life at the same time. Women in ministry spend most of their experiences facing a chronically uphill battle and often deal with lack of cooperation among family, friends, and those who are closest to them.

Doing something radical, different, and establishment-challenging always comes with a price. It's easy for us to look back over history and think about how hard those women had it, but the reality is many women are experiencing the same kind of challenges and trials right now, and they need our support and interest.

If you are a woman connected to a woman in ministry, edify and encourage your leader. Recognize the challenge your leader faces and the unique difficulties that come with being a woman in ministry. Step up and realize she is a history maker, here to do a powerful work in this time and age…and honor her for that.

If you are a woman in ministry yourself, realize how important being in ministry is and how monumental it is to be a woman in ministry, even today. Standing in a pulpit with ordination credentials is a revolutionary act, and doing the work of ministry beyond the pulpit is even more revolutionary. Make a stand for all women in ministry and embrace other women who are also in ministry, realizing you need each other in order to labor for the Gospel all over the world.

- DAILY DISCIPLINE: ATTEND A SERVICE, CONFERENCE, OR EVENT HELD BY A WOMAN IN MINISTRY…AND SUPPORT HER!

- DAY 37 -
Blessed are Those Who Hunger and Thirst for Righteousness

THEY ARE BLESSED WHO HUNGER AND THIRST AFTER JUSTICE [RIGHTEOUSNESS], FOR THEY WILL BE SATISFIED [FILLED].
(MATTHEW 5:6)

• DAILY READING: 1 JOHN 2:24-29

What are you like when you are hungry and thirsty? Whether it's food or drink you seek, you can't think of another thing except food or drink. It gnaws at you and you have a hard time focusing. You aren't into anyone, anything, any new ideas, or any concepts until you are full and thirst has been satisfied, and that is the beginning and the end of the whole matter.

Not too long ago I had a powerful realization because of dealing with someone who wasn't all they claimed to be...or so it seemed to me. Months earlier, we had a long conversation about how wrong it was for the church to treat certain groups of people. I spoke my heart in the discussion, and this individual reiterated what I said, plus some of her own thoughts. When we had someone in the church who fit the description of what we'd discussed, however, her response was quite different than she had indicated in the earlier conversation. She was notably uncomfortable and was notably awkward in her delivery and interaction with this person. From watching her, I came to realize there is a marked difference between feeling something is wrong and having the conviction – the deep hunger and thirsting – to make it right.

It isn't an accident that in the Beatitudes the imagery of hunger and thirsting for righteousness is used to illustrate its point. It's a way of discussing things all of us can understand and realize hungering and thirsting means more than having an opinion about something or hoping something else around them will change. When Jesus talks about hungering and thirsting for righteousness, He is telling us there are always going to be those whose focus is righteousness, and nothing else. They will be people who pursue whatever is right, no matter how

75

difficult it may be, and the Lord promises them that in that pursuit, they will find their fill.

There's a radical difference between observing something to be wrong and wanting to do something to right the wrongs that surround us. This difference, however, is what marks us on different sides and ends of righteousness. It's possible to be an individual who notes wrong in the world but doesn't do much to correct it. We can be individuals who believe in God, who recognize there is much to do in this world, and who even think things should be done, but sit around and wait for someone else to do something about those wrongs rather than taking them on ourselves. It is a disheartening realization to look around the church and see so many people who recognize wrong is around them, but who do not hunger and thirst long enough to see righteousness fulfilled.

What side of righteousness are you on? Pursuing righteousness is something that takes all of us. It's easy to look at the different issues and attitudes present in the church and breeze by them, but it's a lot more lasting of a stand to be someone who treats doing the right thing and living right as if it is as important as food or drink.

- DAILY DISCIPLINE: PURSUE RIGHTEOUSNESS BY WORKING TO FIX THINGS THAT ARE WRONG.

- DAY 38 -
Motherhood and Maternity

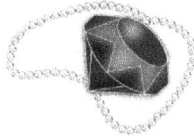

WHY WAS I NOT BURIED [HIDDEN] LIKE A CHILD BORN DEAD [STILLBORN],
LIKE A BABY WHO NEVER SAW THE LIGHT OF DAY?
(JOB 3:16)

- DAILY READING: EXODUS 1:15-22

When we think about childhood mortality and women dying in childbirth, we usually think of colonial home births that were unsterile and without doctors present. We assume that if children die in childhood and women die in childbirth today, it must happen in some remote part of the world where people live in huts with dirt floors. The realities about mortality surrounding childhood and childbirth are much closer to home, although there is no denying that such conditions do exist today.

For every 1,000 babies, about six die during their first year. The top reasons for infant death include birth defects, preterm birth, low birth weight, maternal complications, sudden infant death syndrome (SIDS), and injuries. These causes account for about 57% of all infant deaths in the United States.[8] Worldwide, approximately 830 women die every day from preventable issues related to pregnancy and childbirth.[9] Even in the United States, mortality as a result from childbirth is on the rise. Lack of adequate medical care, medical mistakes, lack of access to hospitals or proper sanitation, and undiagnosed and untreated medical conditions all contribute to an issue that, while might not be often discussed, is most definitely an issue in our modern day and age.

Most people reading this book probably live in nations embroiled in debates about abortion and contraception, and many probably know about protests and diligence projects to shut down organizations who supply contraception or perform abortions within their region. In so doing, many are unaware they are also closing accessible healthcare clinics that rely on government resources to stay open. Closing off these organizations means women will not have affordable access, neither in the United States or in many third-world countries, to ensure healthy pregnancies and proper medical care in such serious and dire circumstances.

It's easy to try and reduce the issues we hear about and care about to singular topics, but the truth behind every issue is there is something else connected to it that suffers if we get so blinded by one position, we start ignoring the bigger picture. If we want women to have healthy babies and children to survive through infancy and childhood, we need to be people who are willing to make sure children don't lose their mothers in childbirth and that both mother and child have access to proper medical care throughout the process and beyond.

Not everyone has the luxury of health insurance. Many working families worldwide are not lazy, are not on any sort of government subsidy, and make sure they work hard to provide for their families. They are worried about food on the table and accessible housing, and unfortunately, medical care is not something accessible nor affordable for these people. Instead of judging people who are unable to have extensive medical care and insurance, make sure that you are not advocating their lack of it by ignoring the truth behind the issues. No mother or baby should die for lack of medical access or proper care.

- DAILY DISCIPLINE: SUPPORT AN ORGANIZATION THAT ADVOCATES HEALTHY PREGNANCIES FOR WOMEN.

- DAY 39 -
Loving our Enemies

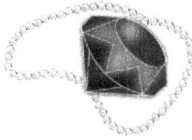

> BUT I SAY TO YOU, LOVE YOUR ENEMIES.
> PRAY FOR THOSE WHO HURT [PERSECUTE] YOU.
> (MATTHEW 5:44)

- DAILY READING: ROMANS 12:17-21

During a Bible study class at Sanctuary International Fellowship Tabernacle – SIFT, the topic of enemies once came up. Along with the topic was an elaborate and fascinating discussion into the concept of what an enemy is and what makes someone an enemy. The question was posed, "Do any of us really have enemies?" to which I had to sit back and think a little bit and mention the topic again during our Sunday service. The Bible is so clear about us loving our enemies, but we know that the major enemy we all have is Satan, who manipulates people and situations to get us into a frenzy and so upset we fail to follow God as we should. The question then becomes, as was posed in Bible study to a certain extent – who is our real enemy?

Satan is certainly the enemy of all enemies, but Satan works through people who willingly submit themselves against the things of God. When someone disobeys God, they become Satan's puppet and thus put themselves into a position to become the enemy of someone else. There are also times when people willingly do things to put themselves first, or do things out of selfish and fleshly ambition, who also become enemies because their intentions and motives do not consider others. This is a little simplistic of an understanding of enemies from a spiritual perspective, and for the sake of space, I am not going to get into a dissertation on spiritual warfare. The reality is that Satan and flesh turn would-be friends into enemies, and cause us to want to lash out, retaliate, or interact with them in a way we ordinarily would never dream of doing.

The Bible doesn't tell us to hate our enemies. The Bible doesn't tell us to be a fool when it comes to our enemies, either, which means we are called to use caution when dealing with others who just don't appear to measure up to who they claim to be. Instead of calling us to hate our enemies, the Bible commands us to love them, to treat and esteem them in the same way we would want to be treated and esteemed, and to desire for them the things that we desire for ourselves. This sounds like a tall and impossible order, especially in the face of someone who has wronged us or who advocates a cause that is opposed to the values we espouse. The automatic response most of us have to our enemies is to wish them harm or death, thinking such will stop their infiltration into the rest of the world to hurt and wrong others.

The reason we are supposed to love our enemies is because evil and wrongdoing is just not this simple. While we associate wrongdoing with our enemies, true spiritual insight recognizes our enemies have a common source, and that is the great enemy, Satan. His defeat alone belongs to Jesus, Who gives all that follow Satan the chance to repent before the hour when Satan is officially and completely destroyed. Jesus won the battle over Satan with love. Love will heal our enemies. Hate will make sure the battle rages on from age to age and person to person.

- DAILY DISCIPLINE: FORGIVE SOMEONE WHO HAS BECOME AN ENEMY.

- DAY 40 -
Clothes for the Naked

I WAS WITHOUT CLOTHES [NAKED], AND YOU GAVE ME SOMETHING TO WEAR [CLOTHED ME]...
(MATTHEW 5:36)

- DAILY READING: JAMES 2:1-7

*I*t's hard to fathom in a world where the clothing and textile industry brought in almost $2,560 trillion dollars in 2010 alone[10] that there are many people who go without clothes or who do not have the ability to provide clothes for their families. Clothing is such a commodity to most that the whole concept of making clothing optional in certain communities (what we used to call nudist camps) has become an industry all its own. The church, in its own way, seems very preoccupied with fashion: how long or short some woman's skirt is, how tight a man's pants are, how low cut a top is, and how fitted a garment is to a person's body. It seems there is no end to the lack of argument, disagreement, or dissention when it comes to attire in church (or in the world, for that matter). Fashion is a big business, and it plays a large role in all our lives, whether we want to admit it, or not.

In ancient times, clothing was seen as an exterior display of someone's wealth. Dress indicated someone's social class and those who were rich were quick to lord their attire over the poor, whose clothing was more minimal. This led to the development of extensive teaching on modesty in the first century, which, believe it or not, had nothing to do with sex or clothing that provoked sexual interest. Biblical modesty related to literally wearing one's income on their sleeves and for the rich to no longer flaunt their wealth in front of the poor, causing class distinction and inequality in the church.

Clothing's basic purpose was, and remains, to protect the human body from the elements. It's a simple item that seeks to keep us secure, warm, protected from physical illness or invasion, and keep us comfortable. The concept we have now of fashion exists as a form of self-expression, something to define and display who we are based on our exterior wear. There are millions worldwide, however, who don't see clothing for this purpose. They are looking for something to keep them warm and dry, no longer exposed to the elements and to help keep their bodies clean. It's not about a label or a designer name, and they certainly hope – and pray – that someone will look down upon their own pitied state and will reach up and help to take away their nakedness.

Those who have been "uncovered" in some way, by rape, sexual assault, sexual abuse, or who are victims of torture also experience the sting of nakedness that requires the softness and protection of those who are willing to help them out through comfort to cover their perceived nakedness.

All of us have clothes we no longer wear, that don't fit us or are no longer "us" anymore. Every one of us can donate our old clothes to a project that helps those who don't have clothing to obtain the clothing they need. Having to stand naked or impoverished before the world is a terrible feeling. Be someone who covers others in love through clothing donations.

- DAILY DISCIPLINE: MAKE A DONATION TO A LOCAL THRIFT STORE OR CLOTHING PROGRAM.

- DAY 41 -

Proclaiming the Year of the Lord's Favor

HE HAS SENT ME TO ANNOUNCE THE TIME WHEN THE LORD WILL SHOW
HIS KINDNESS [YEAR OF THE LORD'S FAVOR; AN ALLUSION TO
THE YEAR OF JUBILEE; LEV. 25:10; LUKE 4:18–19]...
(ISAIAH 61:2)

- DAILY READING: LEVITICUS 25:8-22

A few years ago, I started hearing the expression "Favor ain't fair." I've heard it used in many ways, but it is most typically used to indicate favor is not given to us because of things we've done or because of who we are, but because God is good and chooses to favor us. I don't know if I believe it's fair to say that "favor ain't fair," as if it is something that has no merit to our lives, whatsoever. If we look through the Bible, favor consistently followed people as they followed God's will for their lives, which means it was a manifestation of the good of God working through situations as they partnered with God. Favor was based on their partnership, that promise and purpose, and that brought good things into fruition.

We hear so much doom and gloom from pulpits, news outlets, Christian moves, and Christian sources. They are quick to tell us that the "end is near" and that things are going to "get a lot worse." Many don't offer much promise for things ever improving or getting better. The simple reason for this is because doom and gloom is a quick sell for Christian authors, news outlets, movies, and other forms of media. There are those who are scared by such hype and try very hard to do what they can, right now, and there are those who are tickled by the idea of disorder and destruction. They want those they feel are in error to "get theirs" and they like the idea of torment and torture, especially when people can't escape from it.

I don't deny judgment does exist in the Bible. We see it time and time again for those who willfully turn their backs on God. I don't know if I see a promise of torment and torture, though. What I see as a consistent Biblical message is the promise of hope, one that proclaims a year of God's favor to those both near and far, who can, for an indefinite length of time (as Hebrew terminology is often unspecific when it comes to lengths of time), come forward and work with God to receive that favorable outcome in their lives. It is a God-thing to let people know God loves them and that He wants to do and bring good things into their lives.

Although it is an unpopular message to proclaim, there is nowhere in the Bible that ever tells us to go and preach about hell or hellfire to people. The Bible consistently tells us to proclaim that God is near to people and, as we go, to proclaim the year of His favor. Now is the time we must respond to His promise, and by responding, we all have the opportunity to make this world better, right here, and right now. God doesn't give us His favor to make us feel good about ourselves or to bless us so we can flaunt it in the face of our enemies or of people we don't like very much. His favor is there so we can mobilize the Kingdom of God, go about doing good and proclaiming to others that we have received of this great favor, and they can, too. No matter how many wonderful government initiatives come and go, the only program that shall bring about lasting change here and now is the day of God's favor.

- DAILY DISCIPLINE: INSTEAD OF TALKING ABOUT HELL AND THE DEVIL, PROCLAIM HEAVEN AND THE KINGDOM.

- DAY 42 -

Beyond Borders

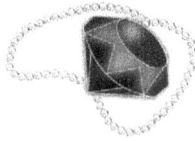

THEY WERE ALL FILLED WITH THE HOLY SPIRIT, AND THEY BEGAN TO SPEAK
DIFFERENT [OTHER; OR FOREIGN] LANGUAGES [TONGUES] BY THE POWER
THE HOLY SPIRIT WAS GIVING THEM [REVERSING THE CONFUSION
OF LANGUAGES AT THE TOWER OF BABEL; GEN. 11:1–9].
(ACTS 2:4)

• DAILY READING: ACTS 2:14-39

When most people think about church, they think of a concept of church that falls into the premise of a building. Church is where you go on a Sunday or Saturday morning to sing songs, hear some preaching, and dress in your best clothes (or something like that). Church is something, in this mindset, that you go to, you attend, and then you leave the church and go home from – away from, leaving behind – only to pick it up again next Sunday.

If we view church in this manner, it severely distorts our concept of true Christianity and what it means to be a Christian. Any of us can go into any house of worship, of any belief system, on any given day, and have whatever goes on in that place have absolutely no effect on us, whatsoever. For example, not too long ago, I took my visiting spiritual daughter to a local Hindu temple to look around and talk to the priests before she went back home. We had a nice time talking to the leaders of the temple and having them answer a few questions for us, and then we left. Going in that Hindu temple didn't make us Hindus. It didn't make us interested in the content of the Hindu religion or have any understanding of what it means to be a Hindu. Yet, it is this kind of mentality – "I go to church!" – that hurts our concept of what it means to be a believer in this world and impact the lives of those around us.

Believe it or not, there are millions of Christians all over the world who, just like you, believe in Jesus Christ and seek to call upon Him and worship Him in spirit and in truth. They, most likely, look different

85

from you. They come from a culture that is far different from yours and that means when they read the Bible, some of the way they read and interpret it is radically different. They probably dress differently and almost always speak a different language. These facts do not change that they are believers who need you as much as you need them in the Body of Christ.

Church is not something that just happens where we are, in a nice, little, neat box on Sunday or Saturday morning. It's who we are, and it is something that is not afraid to cross necessary borders or to reach out to those who are different from us in some obvious way. In the early church, the first believers made it their mission to make sure the Gospel transcended borders and cultures and that as many people as possible could praise the Lord along with them. As a unique facet, it is truly the Gospel of Christ that can transcend nations, cultures, and lives, just by being what God has created it to be.

Everyone wants (and needs) to hear good news the world over. If we are willing to move beyond our comfortable pews, our fashion competitions, our own biases, and our own ideas about what church should be like, we will find an entire world of believers, one by one, who have been transformed by God's grace and are waiting to receive that hand of hope from another believer.

- DAILY DISCIPLINE: SUPPORT A MODERN-DAY MISSIONARY.

- DAY 43 -
A Walk for Justice

THE KING SAID, 'FRIEND, HOW WERE YOU ALLOWED TO COME IN HERE? YOU ARE NOT DRESSED FOR A WEDDING.' BUT THE MAN SAID NOTHING [WAS SPEECHLESS/SILENT].
(MATTHEW 22:12)

- DAILY READING: ROMANS 12:1-8

When I started learning about the Civil Rights Movement, the first thing that caught my eye was the amount of time activists spent walking, up on their feet. They weren't just walking like we walk now for exercise, either. These were men and women who were dressed, very formally at that, walking for miles in their dress shoes and heels. They wore suits and pearls, ties and dress shirts, and stood for something, dressed as professionals, who knew justice was needed and would not sit still for anything. It didn't matter if their feet hurt. It didn't matter if they were tired. It didn't matter if they were hot. They weren't interested in their own comforts, and they knew they had to be the whole part, a positive representation of the movement, to get it to advance forward.

It was the Civil Rights Movement's activists that inspired me to realize how we carry ourselves and what we are willing to do for the causes we claim for our own matter in a most literal sense. We often complain because we feel as if people do not take us seriously when we have a cause, but do we ever think about how we represent ourselves when it is time to represent what we stand for? Many of us say we want change, and we want people to see what we are saying, but how serious are we about that statement? Are we willing to walk, willing to march, willing to dress the part and look the part for what we believe in? If we aren't, then what we say we want to happen will never come to pass because we won't be taken seriously. If we don't take what we believe in seriously, neither will anyone else.

Those who advocated for change at the tumultuous crossroads of the Civil Rights Era did so at a cost to themselves. They had to travel long distances, donate financially to keep the cause going, and keep going when they were hungry, tired, or maybe uninterested in doing the same thing over and over again. Many had families that had to survive without their presence and many more had to forsake relationships or things they wanted personally for the sake of the cause.

The extensive physical toll Civil Rights leaders took by walking far distances and having to be on their feet was just the beginning of the sacrifices individuals had to make to win the battle for civil rights. Where are you with your own beliefs and causes? One of the biggest differences we see in many today is an unwillingness to do something or make a stand if it means they can't have something else in their lives. Yes, life is a matter of making choices and standing behind them, but freedom and truth are waiting for those in this generation who are ready, willing, and able to make the sacrifices needed to bring the change we say we want, but many are unwilling to stand up and achieve.

Remember yourself when it is time to stand up for something. Remember the ancestors who have gone before…and put on your pearls, heels, and shoes to show up!

- DAILY DISCIPLINE: MAKE A POINT TO "DRESS THE PART" NEXT TIME YOU ARE READY TO STAND UP FOR SOMETHING!

- DAY 44 -
Becoming Brave

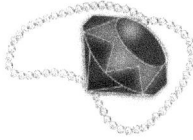

I CAN DO ALL THINGS THROUGH CHRIST, BECAUSE HE [THE ONE WHO]
GIVES ME STRENGTH.
(PHILIPPIANS 4:13)

- DAILY READING: EPHESIANS 6:10-20

*I*n the blockbuster movie *The Help*, the lead character, Skeeter (whose real name is Eugenia), writes a book based on a series of interviews done with African-American maids in her hometown of Jackson, Mississippi during the Civil Rights era (1963). The book rocked the world in more ways than one and took the courage of conviction for Skeeter to walk away from friends, a fiancé, and social prestige in her southern town. In one particular scene toward the end of the movie, her mother says to her, "Sometimes courage skips a generation." By saying this, her mother was telling her she didn't have the bravery, nor the courage of conviction, to stand up and do something about the racism and societal injustices that surrounded her. From watching the movie, we can see the mother was interested in being a socialite, and racism was such an integrated part of social society in those days she was not brave enough to stand against social acceptability even though she knew what was going on was wrong.

It would be nice to assume that wrong doesn't live in our world anymore. After all, we claim to be more enlightened, tolerant, and understanding than generations past, but the realities exist that there is plenty of wrong going on right under the surfaces of enlightenment, tolerance, and understanding. Part of our call as individuals who do the work of ministry and who live the Gospel is to see through the things in this world that paint a comfortable veneer over the wrong that exists in this world. The only way we can do that – and do what needs to be done in change – is to stand up in bravery.

We often think of bravery as taking the form of running into a burning building to save a child or of being willing to stand on the front lines of a physical battle as one sacrifices their lives for the cause. Bravery doesn't just look like this, as hard as it might be to imagine. Bravery takes the form whenever someone is willing to change a paradigm, all by oneself, without any validation or help from anyone else to bring that change to pass. Bravery is seen on the face of a domestic violence victim who walks out of their situation. It is seen in the actions of someone who stands up to a bully in the schoolyard. Bravery is seen in every person who walks away from drugs or alcohol, for good, to face reality head-on. It is seen in a million different ways and a million different faces, through people who are willing to put one foot in front of another and do what they know is right, unequivocally, in each and every situation they find themselves in.

Bravery is not easy. We live in a conforming world that falls into the category of the mother in the movie mentioned earlier. Social conformities and acceptability exist on the precept that people won't be brave and won't step out to do the right thing. That's why it's such a revolutionary thing to be a true believer: social conformities or not, bravery is a part of who we are, and a part of who we want to become.

- DAILY DISCIPLINE: STEP OUT AND DO THE RIGHT THING.

- DAY 45 -
Blessed are the Merciful

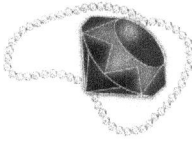

THEY ARE BLESSED WHO SHOW MERCY TO OTHERS, FOR GOD WILL SHOW
MERCY TO THEM [THEY WILL BE SHOWN MERCY; THE PASSIVE VERB IMPLIES
GOD AS SUBJECT].
(MATTHEW 5:7)

- DAILY READING: HEBREWS 8:7-13

One of the most difficult things to live with throughout life is the awareness that you have done something to someone else and they refuse to forgive you for it. Maybe more difficult than this is the realization you have had nothing more than a misunderstanding with someone and they still refuse to talk to you again or to reconcile the situation. Standing on a principle that they have been wronged, they would rather destroy a relationship, a contact, a friendship, a connection, than honestly walk in a principle of kindness and forgiveness.

The truth about being merciful is it's a concept foreign to us in the being of our fleshly nature. We want to be right, we want others to recognize we are right, and we don't like the idea that we have been wronged or offended. If people have wronged us, even if it is in the form of a misunderstanding, we want to be raised up as the victors, because being victorious means someone else must be below where we are. We expect our friends as well as our enemies to regard us in a certain way, and when that situation comes along to challenge that notion, we become more and more irate and angry with that individual.

Being merciful, however, is a principle by which we treat others with kindness and forgiveness, giving relief of suffering and alienation through compassion. Mercy, as we discussed in an earlier devotion, is not necessarily something we might deserve, but it is most definitely something we need. As people, we don't get it right all the time, even in our interactions with others. No matter how hard we try, things don't always turn out the way we might like. The more frustrated we become, the more inclined we are to lash out or interact with others in a manner that displays our true frustrations. It doesn't mean it's how we always really feel about something, but it is definitely a side of us that comes out, rearing its ugly head, time and time again when we wish it would not.

If we are merciful to those who have these moments, quick to walk in a place full of mercy and understanding, then we too will receive mercy when we have our moments. What we give to others is what we will receive in return, if as nothing more than a spiritual principle from our Father in Heaven. Giving mercy leads to mercy and leads us to others who desire to embody the principle of mercy in their own lives. When we walk in mercy, we will find it, and we will more readily recognize the need for change within ourselves.

In being called to mercy, we are not just called to like it or think about it. We are called to merciful, so full of mercy that it displays in all the things we desire to do for others: through compassion, right action, right speech, and right purpose. Mercy, whether we want to admit it or not, has the power to change our whole lives. It starts when we are willing to extend it to someone else, no matter how wronged we feel.

- DAILY DISCIPLINE: EXERCISE KINDNESS AND FORGIVENESS, EVEN WHEN IT'S HARD.

- DAY 46 -
Hope for the Offended

IF YOUR FELLOW BELIEVER [BROTHER (OR SISTER)] SINS AGAINST YOU,
GO AND TELL HIM WHAT HE DID WRONG [REPROVE/CONVICT/CORRECT HIM]
IN PRIVATE [BETWEEN YOU AND HIM ALONE]. IF HE LISTENS TO YOU,
YOU HAVE HELPED THAT PERSON TO BE YOUR BROTHER OR SISTER AGAIN
[GAINED/WON BACK YOUR BROTHER (OR SISTER)].
(MATTHEW 18:15)

- DAILY READING: 1 CORINTHIANS 10:23-33

One of the greatest issues I see present in the modern-day church is the way we have turned offense and being offended into a sin. Because we emphasize interpersonal connection over the reality that some people might not be right for us and the need to disconnect at times, we are creating new bondages for victims as we make offense – a life fact that happens sometimes – seem wrong or demonic. In fact, I find "offense" to be treated as if it is the worst possible sin imaginable (when it's not even a sin). People act as if being offended will hold you back from your entire life's future, from being anything anywhere in time, and that God will punish you from disconnecting from others who have, in some way, wronged you.

I believe strongly in forgiveness; I also believe we need to act in wisdom and use good judgment when it comes to areas of offense in our lives. Yes, there are people who use offense as an excuse to be in control or to avoid reality, but the sad truth about offense is that it often comes along in situations where it is quite justified. We are human beings who live in a fallen, sinful world where others sometimes seek to attack the integrity, dignity, and image of God present within another person and experiencing that wound is something that hurts beyond measure. It takes the work of God, a deep sense of forgiveness, and a deep need for distance to heal the hurts of offense so that a person can feel whole again.

As much as people like to victimize victims all over again (as a running theme within our culture), living with offense is a difficult and painful thing that stands as a constant reminder of whatever was done to someone to cause them the deep hurt, anger, or sadness that results from the wrong that was done to them. We forget our actions have consequences, and doing something offensive, deemed as improper or wrong to someone else, does still matter. When someone is offended because we have behaved unseemly or when we ourselves are offended because someone has behaved improperly toward us, there is justification in being upset or hurt.

Rather than condemning offense, the Scriptures promise that those who are offended shall find their hope, their healing, and their restoration. That process to restoration, healing, and hope can begin a lot easier if the offender in such a situation is ready and willing to leave their gift at the altar, stop insisting they were right about whatever they did or stop brushing it off as not being "that bad" and pull themselves together to go and apologize. Even if reconciliation never takes place, admittance of wrong goes a long way to setting someone else right.

If you have been wronged, you might never get that apology. Whether it comes or not, God has a promise for you: you shall hope again, you shall live again, and a day shall come when you do not hurt again. It is vital we hold onto that, even if it seems impossible.

- DAILY DISCIPLINE: MAKE AMENDS WITH SOMEONE YOU HAVE WRONGED.

- DAY 47 -
Creative Support

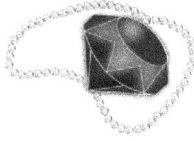

[THEREFORE; SO THEN] WHEN WE HAVE THE OPPORTUNITY TO HELP
[DO GOOD TO] ANYONE, WE SHOULD DO IT. BUT WE SHOULD GIVE SPECIAL
ATTENTION [ESPECIALLY] TO THOSE WHO ARE IN THE FAMILY [HOUSEHOLD]
OF BELIEVERS [FAITH].
(GALATIANS 6:10)

- DAILY READING: ACTS 20:32-36

When we think about supporting someone, we often think about doing it through our own personal finances. If we think about support through group events, our first thoughts are usually of bake sales or other means to try and raise necessary funds to help or empower whoever it might be that is in need. Because we think in terms of our own culture and our own experience, we always automatically think the answer to someone's problems is money: more of it, plenty of it, and purposes for it.

The truth about money is that nobody is going to turn it down, especially when it stares at them right in the face. But when it comes to supporting other people, there are many ways we can support others without giving money all the time. There are also lots of instances where it may not be money that is truly needed as a form of support. If we always use money to try and fix everything, we are missing opportunities to do great things for others that money cannot buy.

Support, as we often call it, is a part of the gift of edification in the church. In this world and especially in churches today, there is a severe spirit of competition and aggression that causes people to be isolated and alienated unto themselves. If someone feels they have a gift or comes to a place where they discover a calling, they will, most likely, face a great deal of opposition in bringing those things to fruition. Leaders are afraid someone else will overthrow them, others deal with jealousy and envy, and people tend to feel like they are going through everything alone.

Sometimes people don't need a check; sometimes they need a hug. Sometimes they need a listening ear. Sometimes they just need someone to be there for them. If you know of someone who is doing work in ministry and having an event, they need you to go out and support them instead of waiting for the video to post on the internet. Sometimes someone needs an encouraging word or you to keep your promise to assist or volunteer in some way.

We've started using money to create a distance between us and others, as well as between us and the problems others have. We give money because it's easy, because it's a way to say we have done something and be done with it. If we can't give financially, we think that nullifies our responsibility to do anything at all and makes it so we feel we step away with a clean conscience, when we are not. Money or not, we are called to do something by God to support others in our lives.

The message we should be getting here is that support means giving of yourself, not just writing a check and hoping someone will be all right to fend for themselves. We cannot claim to be in the Body and be so disconnected that we do not care about, nor take interest, in the true needs that others have. It might seem hard or awkward to reach out, but in the long run, doing so will better someone's life far more than if we keep throwing money from a distance.

- DAILY DISCIPLINE: SUPPORT A CAUSE, MINISTRY, OR SITUATION WITHOUT GIVING MONEY.

- Day 48 -

Speak up for Those Who Cannot Speak for Themselves

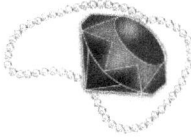

SPEAK UP [OPEN YOUR MOUTH] FOR THOSE WHO CANNOT SPEAK FOR
THEMSELVES; DEFEND THE RIGHTS OF ALL THOSE WHO HAVE NOTHING
[VULNERABLE/FRAGILE PEOPLE].
(PROVERBS 31:8)

- DAILY READING: 1 THESSALONIANS 5:12-25

*I*n the United States a public defender is provided for an accused criminal, even if they cannot afford their own defense team. This sounds good, but if we look at the system as a whole, the reality of public defense takes on a whole nature of politics most people would like to pretend do not really exist. Often poorer individuals who are accused of committing crimes get poor representation, are persuaded into taking deals that aren't really "deals" at all or who are pushed into pleas or admittances of guilt when they are not really guilty. The state of our court system strongly bespeaks the reality that justice is infrequently found and that poorer individuals do not have the same chance of victory in the system as a wealthy person does.

In Biblical times, the poor experienced a similarly unjust fate. If they were in need or classified as poor and were accused of something, they did not have the means or social status to defend themselves properly. There was also the issue of social protection that simply did not exist for the poor because they were unable to bribe or buy someone off to accomplish what needed to be done. The inequalities of sinful societies made it, so the poor had to bear injustice without consideration for them as human beings.

The concept of speaking up for someone who cannot speak for themselves indicates an individual's voice has been stolen from them for some social or societal reason. There are many instances of people who have their voice and sense of self stolen by society: rape victims, those who are poor, those who are abused, those who live in captivity, those who are wrongly convicted of a crime, and those who are marginalized by society due to differences all experience the sting of being unable to stand up for themselves.

God calls us to be people who believe in right, even if it isn't societally comfortable. This is a deep challenge to Christianity today, as it has become society has linked Christianity of all denominations with social status and social prestige. Going to the big church and giving a lot of money on Sunday is associated with being a good citizen and even socially generous. It also means doing that creates connections for jobs and for social involvements that look just as prestigious. Doing this, however, doesn't mean one properly understands the Christian walk or sets up connections that relate to lasting justice.

As Christians, we are called to love our neighbor, which means we want for our neighbor what we want for ourselves. If someone is in a situation where they cannot speak up for their own rights, we should be people who care enough about them and about their situation to speak up on their behalf. We can't say we love somebody and then let them experience wrong, no matter what form it comes in. Speaking up for others gives us a sense of justice and balance in a manner that does not come from remaining silent and hoping matters will resolve themselves.

- DAILY DISCIPLINE: SPEAK OUT FOR EQUAL RIGHTS FOR ALL ON SOCIAL MEDIA.

- DAY 49 -
Don't Fear New Experiences

PLANT EARLY IN THE MORNING, AND WORK UNTIL [DO NOT LET YOUR HAND REST AT] EVENING, BECAUSE YOU DON'T KNOW IF THIS OR THAT WILL SUCCEED. THEY MIGHT BOTH DO WELL.
(ECCLESIASTES 11:6)

- DAILY READING: MATTHEW 6:25-34

What is your morning routine like? For millions of people, it probably involves a morning beverage (such as coffee or tea), maybe a morning workout, a quick check on the television or internet for the daily weather or morning commute, a shower, some breakfast, proper attire, and then off to work. It doesn't matter that many hate their jobs or have other dreams, because their fear of the unknown and doing something new, in the form of a new experience, scares them too much to break out of the ordinary routine.

We hear stories about brave individuals who get so tired and bored with their average routine that they take an incredible risk to go somewhere else in their lives. The stories we love the best are those of successes, who stood somewhere with nothing, doing without things, and risking it all to get where they are today. Had they not taken that leap, they wouldn't be successful, rich, or happy in their lives. They, fortunately, found everything they hoped and dreamed of finding because of taking that chance and doing something new.

The stories we don't tend to like are those of people who risked it all and lost in their attempts for a new life. There are stories of people who risked it all, lost their shirts, and as a result, went back to the life they knew all along. They tried something new and because it didn't bring about the results they desired, they went back to what they knew because it was easier. They tried, they failed, and now they are afraid to do something else.

For every success story we hear there are several other stories behind that one individual where they tried something and failed.

There are also many other smaller testimonials and experiences where someone tried something as a part of a bigger plan that didn't work out, thus requiring them to try something else in its place.

We all have the same choice that successful people have: try something new or walk away and do what we already know. It's easy to look at someone else's life and think they have it all or that they had certain opportunities or experiences that we don't, but the reality is that what success and failure often come down to is the willingness to keep trying new things and have new experiences. What we fear in new experiences is that sense of the unknown, of not knowing what the outcome of what we will find or what might happen. This shakes our sense of security, which makes us want to hold on to that which is comfortable – and sometimes mundane or even miserable – all the more.

If you want to be someone who makes a difference in this world, you can't fear change. Change starts with each one of us and our willingness to do something different or try something new. The world, this life, our hope and promise are all full of experiences that are waiting to be had and known but will only be known if we are willing to see success even in failure and move forward to a new promise.

- DAILY DISCIPLINE: TRY SOMETHING NEW THAT YOU HAVE ALWAYS WANTED TO DO.

- DAY 50 -
A Fairer Kind of Trade

INVEST YOUR MONEY IN FOREIGN TRADE, AND ONE OF THESE DAYS YOU WILL
MAKE A PROFIT.
(ECCLESIASTES 11:1, GNT)

- DAILY READING: ECCLESIASTES 11:1-6

Christopher Columbus was long taught to be a hero in the American classroom. He was credited with "discovering America" and with being the first European to realize the earth was round and not flat. We were taught he was a man with vision who had to fight and claw his way to prove his point. What we didn't know about Christopher Columbus was that he was involved in the slave trade, he and his men brought disease to the Native Americans to which they were not immune, and he was certainly not the first European to realize the earth was round rather than flat. He was also not the first European to visit the Americas. What he was, however, is a glaring picture of the way in which we do not properly tackle the topic of economic trade throughout history.

Slavery. Theft. Dishonesty. Rape. Oppression. Mistreatment. Abuse. What do all these words have in common? They are all part of the history of economic trade worldwide. In many ways, these things still exist as a part of economic trade and economic maintenance in the world today. In response to arguments that historical trends of trade create slaves rather than economic sustainability, a movement known as fair trade emerged back in 1997. When a product is fair trade certified, it means the items come from developing countries and the workers involved in the production of those goods are treated fairly, ethically, and paid properly. The history of trade has not always been fair, but fair trade seeks to turn the tide by proving that products can be bought and sold without coming at a cost to those who work in farming or product production.

Fair trade products include coffee, chocolate, wine, fruit, and handmade or personally made goods. When it comes to marketing these different items, fair trade products are controlled by different cooperatives who make decisions about where the products are sold, the volume of the products, and how the money generated by sales are spent among the group. Many social projects result from fair trade profits, including schools, paying teacher's salaries, building new bridges, providing electricity, improving roads and building healthcare facilities. By creating the fair trade system, people all over the world are reaping the benefits of teamwork, economic fairness, fair trade, and seeing to it that employees are paid fair and substantial wages for their hard labor and work.

Whenever you buy an item that is labeled "fair trade certified" you are providing a better life for people in other countries who need the opportunity to profit from crops and labor rather than seeing that profit handed to big corporations who exploit smaller workers. While the system is certainly not perfect, fair trade opens the door to a world of equity in business and profit in a way that not only benefits an individual, but benefits entire communities and groups of people, as well.

- DAILY DISCIPLINE: EXAMINE THE PRODUCTS YOU BUY AND SWITCH TO AT LEAST TWO FAIR TRADE CERTIFIED ITEMS.

- DAY 51 -

Proclaiming the Day of Vengeance

HE HAS SENT ME TO ANNOUNCE... THE TIME WHEN OUR GOD WILL PUNISH
EVIL PEOPLE [DAY OF VENGEANCE OF OUR GOD].
(ISAIAH 61:2)

- DAILY READING: REVELATION 20:11-15

*I*n predominately Muslim countries a principle exists known as "honor killing." In an honor killing, a family member who has somehow brought suggested shame or disgrace to a family or a family lineage must be killed by another family member to restore the concept or idea of whatever their family name represented prior. Things done in the name of honor do not just relate to physical murder, however. There are instances of acid attacks, where chemical acid is thrown on a person's face or genital area to make sure that such an individual will never be eligible for marriage, employment, or life in general. There are also many instances of physical assaults, battery and beatings which many, in many instances, leave a person disfigured for life.

When we think of the word "vengeance," this is the type of thing that we think of: people taking action against someone else for no reason except to try and right whatever they feel that person did that was wrong. As a result, we associate vengeance with some of the highest levels of sin against one's neighbor imaginable. Vengeance is one of those topics we don't like to hear about, whether we are at church or whether we are dealing with something general in our lives. The concept of something "coming with a vengeance" implies great violence or force, and it indicates that whatever is coming comes with a tide that cannot be stopped. Vengeance is thought to be something uncontrollable and undisciplined, something that, on a human level, represents unstoppable anger, something that causes destruction and harm.

The concept of vengeance, however, in its primary definition is one of retribution for a wrong that was done, not uncontrollable anger or aggression vetted on an individual in disgrace or frustration. Vengeance is righting a wrong by doing something or inflicting some sort of judgment against others. And believe it or not, the concept of vengeance, or having every wrong made right, is a Biblical principle. There is just one catch when it comes to vengeance, however, that makes most people very uncomfortable: vengeance is not to be sought out by human means or methods. It is not our place to try and right things on our own, because the realities of hurt and offense are that there is never anything that undoes what was first done to us. Nothing that we do will ever take away the feeling of wrong and will just inflict more pain and hurt in this world in different ways.

The Bible teaches us that vengeance belongs to God Himself, and that He will repay, or make every wrong right in His time. When working and seeing the hurts of the world, we proclaim this day of vengeance – the principle that God will handle every enemy and every wrong done against us and against others, and will right every situation, because He is that good and that amazing of a Savior…unlike any other.

- DAILY DISCIPLINE: TAKE GOD'S WORDS SERIOUSLY AND JUDGE YOURSELF.

- DAY 52 -

Man's Inhumanity to Man

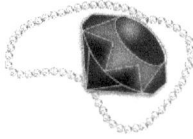

ANYONE WHO KIDNAPS SOMEONE AND EITHER SELLS HIM AS A SLAVE
OR STILL HAS HIM WHEN HE IS CAUGHT [HE IS FOUND IN HIS HAND] MUST BE
PUT TO DEATH.
(EXODUS 21:16)

- DAILY READING: REVELATION 18:11-17

Grace was a Nigerian girl who attended school until she was in the tenth grade. After this, she was sent to work to help support her impoverished family. She did various jobs until she was raped and gave birth to her child, a son. Her father then told her that she was, as a woman, "predestined by God to save her family from poverty by going to Europe to earn money." She was introduced by her father to a woman whose sister lived in Germany. She was told that if she went to Germany, she would have to repay the travel costs and then could work as a babysitter or in a restaurant in Europe to send money back home. She underwent a spiritual ceremony committing to giving back the money, and that she would repay all debts. Grace was then transported along with several other women to Germany with a fake passport, right into the hands of a brothel madam. Even though she tried to get support from her family, they refused to send her home and forced her to remain in submission to the brothel owner. She worked for seven months, forced to have unprotected sex with clients, living without papers and without rights. After a brothel raid, German police detained her, and a hospital examination discovered she had AIDS.[11]

Every year, thousands of men, women, and children fall victim to the world of human trafficking. By abusing power, kidnapping people, abducting individuals or exploiting men and women who are unable to read, human trafficking results in sexual exploitation, forced prostitution, forced labor, slavery, or the removal of body organs in order to profit the huge appetites, immoralities, and thefts of the black market.[12] According to current statistics, there are at least 21 million victims of human trafficking worldwide, with 68% of them in forced labor, 26% are children, and 55% are female.[13] Globally, the average cost of a slave is just $90, and there are at least 20 million slaves in the word today.[14]

We watch things on television documentaries about girls who disappear in foreign countries, never to be seen again. We can look over these things and easily think human trafficking is something going on somewhere else, but not where we live. It's a mistake to think that human trafficking only happens in third world nations or in poor countries, although it certainly does happen there. In the United States, an estimated one out of five runaways reported to the National Center for Missing and Exploited Children were likely sex trafficking victims, and over 27,000 total cases of human trafficking have been reported in the last eight years.[15]

We cannot brush off human trafficking as something that happens to someone else. It happens due to man's sin against mankind, still attempting to enslave and exploit others. As people, we should know where our products come from, the labor involved in their production, and most importantly, how we can best reach out to victims of human trafficking through activism and support.

- DAILY DISCIPLINE: TAKE A CLASS OR EDUCATIONAL SEMINAR ON HUMAN TRAFFICKING.

- DAY 53 -

He Must Increase, but I Must Decrease

He must become greater [increase], and I must become
less important [decrease].
(John 3:30)

- DAILY READING: GALATIANS 2:17-21

Missions. Breast cancer. Mental illness. HIV awareness. Bible
and literature distribution. Alzheimer's. ALS. Premature
babies. Human trafficking. Domestic violence. Education.
Gun control. Ending violence. Healthcare for women. Suicide
prevention. Veteran's affairs. This short list reflects only a handful of
the many varied causes in existence that require assistance, funding, and
volunteers to keep their research and advocacy open and available to
others. It's obvious there is no shortage of places to reach out, to get
involved, and to do great things with if we are only willing to open our
eyes, stop seeing ourselves everywhere we look, and do something great
for someone else.

One of the major complaints I receive from people is they don't
feel as if they are doing anything good with their lives. They go to work,
they might go to church or take on night school or classes, they have
their families, and things are going well...except they don't feel like
they are making a difference in anyone else's lives. They watch the news
on television, they see documentaries about problems that exist, and
even though they know that things are going on, they don't know what
to do about them or where to start with helping out with the world's
problems.

The simplest spiritual principle to finding ways to do good for
others is He must increase, but I must decrease. What this means for us
is that whenever our lives and the different expressions and extensions
of ourselves are our primary focus, we are not ever going to see our
way to do something for someone else. Sure, we might make our focus
on family, on doing good for ourselves, on working so we can get that

promotion and that new car or house sound altruistic, but at the root of it may very well be busying ourselves with extensions of us, reflections of us, and thoughts of us so the entire world around us will see…only…us. The result? People will fuss and tell us how wonderful we are, how sacrificial we are, and encourage us to keep serving ourselves.

Having a job is necessary for survival. There is nothing wrong with wanting to have a family. Within certain boundaries, there isn't even anything wrong with wanting to live in a safer neighborhood or have a car that doesn't break down all the time. There is something wrong with the pursuit of these things because they are a part of us, and we want others to see and notice them to relate back to us how wonderful we are.

If we want to do for others and we want to better the lives of other people, we have to decrease our desire and want to better ourselves and be known and praised for the things that we do. We must be willing to let God work within us, for His nature and glory to shine through our actions and to guide us to organizations and activism that will truly benefit the Kingdom and bless His Name. He must become greater, more prominent, and more relevant, and we, ourselves, become less.

- DAILY DISCIPLINE: BE A PART OF SOMETHING GOOD AND USEFUL THAT HAS NOTHING TO DO WITH YOUR FAMILY OR HOUSEHOLD.

- DAY 54 -
Looking After the Sick

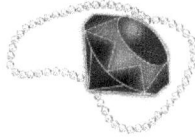

...I WAS SICK AND YOU TOOK CARE OF ME...
(MATTHEW 25:36, GNT)

- DAILY READING: JEREMIAH 30:12-17

Most of us probably don't know that in ancient times, care for the sick was intimately tied to religion. In ancient cultures, people believed their diseases were cured by various deities and were tied to various religious rites and rituals performed in temples. Different cultures ran projects for the poor and needy, and in different parts of the world, travelling religious leaders and practitioners would go from village to village to heal the sick and bring about better living.

In those days, they had no concept about proper hygiene, contamination, germs, or the root of so many illnesses. They were simple and uncomplicated, believing if people were willing to do whatever the gods wanted, they could have the restored healing they sought. The darker side of this (which might sound simplistic and cartoonish to many) was that illness was frequently thought to be a curse, or alienation, from the gods for different things. A punishment for sin or wrongdoing, believing such about the sick led to mistreatment and alienation of sick people who were believed to be bad luck and cursed by God. So even though ancient religion had means by which sick people could be "cured" within their religious understanding, caring for the sick wasn't something that most people were too eager to do.

These attitudes about illness and affliction were an intimate part of Jewish understanding in the first century. Surrounded by pagan influences for thousands of years, the Jews also believed illness was a blight from God and something to be avoided. Healing was a big deal because it restored a person to wholeness, undoing whatever curse they had incurred due to their own sin or to the sins of someone else. The sick were, by virtue of their illness, judged and cast in a certain light; as sinners with a visible result, the product of some sort of unfaithfulness before God, now unveiled before the entire world to see. Nobody wanted a part in that, nobody wanted to touch that, and nobody wanted association with that.

This means Jesus' instruction to His people to take care of the sick, seeing they are comfortable and looked after, was a very revolutionary message for His time. He did not encourage them, nor us, to look after the sick with the motive they will get healed (although it is fine to pray and believe for someone's healing). We were told to look after the sick as a duty, a purpose by which we can give something to someone who cannot repay us. By so doing, Jesus confirmed that many of our fears about contracting disease from others and working with others who are sick are, indeed, unfounded. Helping the sick will not make us sick and it will not transmit someone else's sin or misfortune to us in the process, either.

Sickness in this world is a part of sin, but that doesn't mean people committed a specific sin to become sick. It means they live in a fallen world with fallen people and in compassion, we need to desire to help others who are hurting and in need.

- DAILY DISCIPLINE: VISIT A NURSING HOME OR A SHUT-IN WHO BELONGS TO YOUR CHURCH.

- Day 55 -
Put Your Money Where Your Mouth is!

- **Daily Reading: 2 Corinthians 9:1-15**

All of us have seen the different television commercials full of starving children or impoverished individuals seeking funds to send them to school or to feed them. Most commercials tell us if we are willing to send so much money per month, we can do so much for someone who experiences lack in their lives. They'll even break down how much the offering they request is per day, comparing it to less than a cup of coffee or a newspaper. Their goal is to make you realize that by giving a small amount of money per day, you can make a huge difference in someone's life in the long run.

I don't believe money is everything, as I have stated in earlier devotions. I think sometimes we want to write someone a check and think our duty to do something for someone else is done, hoping money will take care of things for us. I can't deny, though, that sometimes we look at different causes and say we'll pray, or we will support it by liking it on Facebook or another social network without considering that every work that's out there requires financial support to keep it going.

We need to not just be activists who look on and think a cause is right; we need to be activists with our giving. Whenever someone tells us to "Put your money where your mouth is!" it means that we should never say that we believe in something or support something if we aren't supporting it financially. It is an echo of the Biblical principle that wherever our treasure is, there is our heart, as well. If we say we believe in something, whether it's church, ministry, or a cause, but we spend all our money on a car, a house, rent, clothes, vacations, our families, or ourselves, that tells us right then and there that our hearts are really with all of those things and not truly with the things we claim are most important in our lives. Our money tells all our secrets, and it tells everyone what is most important to us, where our hearts are, and what we need to do.

It's natural to understand we can't support every single cause that is out there, and we should not feel guilty every time we watch a television commercial or when we have to say no, we are not able to support something. This does not nullify us from our commitment to support something near and dear to us, something we know makes a difference in the world and that needs our proper support. All of us need to know the value of a dollar and see our giving in the context of something we spend every day or regularly, something that we could do for ourselves, but are choosing to do for someone else because our giving needs to be as real as our endorsement or acclaimed support for some purpose or cause.

God commands us to give of our time, talent, and treasure, which means giving is three-fold. We can't eliminate the financial aspect of giving and call ourselves givers, because it ignores a vital aspect of how we give of ourselves as people. Giving is a whole package…so get out the debit card or checkbook…and start your giving!

- DAILY DISCIPLINE: SOW A FINANCIAL SEED WILLINGLY, WITHOUT BEING ASKED.

- DAY 56 -
The Social Call of the Pastor: Corporal Compassion

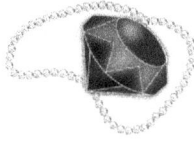

THEN I WILL GIVE YOU NEW RULERS [SHEPHERDS] WHO WILL BE FAITHFUL
TO ME [ACCORDING TO MY HEART], WHO WILL LEAD [SHEPHERD] YOU
WITH KNOWLEDGE AND UNDERSTANDING [INSIGHT].
(JEREMIAH 3:15)

- DAILY READING: MATTHEW 25:31-46

When most of us think of the term "pastor," we think of people (usually men before anyone else) who were the main preachers in the local churches where we grew up. We knew them as prolific orators, able to take a few verses of Scripture and turn them into a service. If you went to a church with a solid children's program, you might even meet the pastor for a few minutes before the main service or before departing for Sunday School or Children's Church. They were people we associated with pulpit work: with doing the work of the Sunday morning worship service and with expounding the Bible so we could all understand it.

The truth about pastors, however, is that pastoral work goes far beyond the comforts of Sunday morning preaching. The word "pastor" means "shepherd," which means the pastoral work takes its inspiration from the work of shepherds. Studying the work of the ancient (and in some parts of the world, modern) shepherd gives us great insight into just what a pastor is called to do and how they are called to execute their work. Shepherds spend a great deal of time knowing their sheep, even naming them and recognizing their individual personalities and attributes. They lived apart from general society because they spent so much time attending to the movements and needs of their sheep. Sheep tend to be stubborn, so the shepherd must think ahead of the sheep who might get themselves into trouble and edge them along, making sure they do for their own good what they don't want to do for themselves. Susceptible to insects and pests, shepherds take time to anoint their sheep, so the bugs and pests won't get to them. The feeding, care, and work of sheep requires the devotion of that shepherd as they attend to their natural needs.

True pastors engage themselves in the very life of their congregations, making sure the needs of the congregants are met. Yes, pastors are there for spiritual needs, but the primary job of a pastor is to feed and meet the needs that exist among a congregation. This means there are physical needs that are a part of congregation responsibility as much as emotional and spiritual needs, as well. True pastors see the relevance in feeding programs, clean water outreach, clothing programs, homeless outreach, care for the sick and elderly, prison ministry, counseling, and hospitality. If a church does not have enough members to maintain programs like these in their own congregations, then a pastor with God's shepherding vision will see to it that they join with social programs or other outreach organizations and help to bring these different things to pass.

We often like to think the world's problems can be solved if we will only be spiritual enough and approach things from a spiritual perspective. It's great and important to be spiritual, and it is a part of solving the world's problems, but the social call of the pastor reminds all of us that some of the world's problems can only be solved if we tackle them head-on…and solve them.

- DAILY DISCIPLINE: SUPPORT THE WORK OF THE LOCAL CHURCH BY ASSISTING IN A SOCIAL OUTREACH MINISTRY.

- DAY 57 -
Toppling Politics

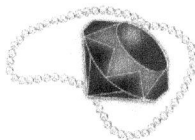

BUT OUR HOMELAND [OR CITIZENSHIP] IS IN HEAVEN, AND WE ARE WAITING FOR OUR SAVIOR, THE LORD JESUS CHRIST, TO COME FROM HEAVEN. (PHILIPPIANS 3:20)

- DAILY READING: MATTHEW 22:17-21

Most Evangelicals believe if the "right candidates" get in office, Christian values will be upheld in the United States and there will be a return to the churchy-mindset of an ordered and purposed world. They believe if the laws are as strict and strident as possible, then people will not fall to crime and that will reduce the incidents of crime in our country. Whether or not this is true remains up for debate, depending on who you're speaking with at the time, but lack of influence on American politics has sent many Evangelicals to other parts of the world to try and influence government spending and ideals. The result has become an influx of laws and rules that severely impede spending and funding from reaching those who need it most. Coupled with government corruption, the influence of Evangelical ideals has created situations where women's clinics do not receive the necessary funding to stay open, women die in childbirth or pregnancy, men do not receive proper healthcare, HIV spreads like wildfire without proper preventative methods, and individuals who are suspected to be gay or lesbian are killed for no other reason at all.

Many people think government involvement is the answer to bringing about needed change or ideals, but the reality is that government politics often cause those most in need to miss out on whatever it is they can receive. Even in a society where it seems like all have the right to participate or provide input, politics wind up in the hands of the most corrupt. Built upon ideals and influences, politics are not a pure game. They involve money, spending, time and effort, and savvy politicians make sure whatever it is that you want to hear is exactly what they say right at the right time.

Hoping for a vote or a candidate to fix what's wrong within a culture or a society is an endless hope. It is also contrary to what God has told us to do as His people. If we are called to be salt and light to the world, that means we are called to do something, not to hope that elected officials will take care of matters for us and tie things up in a nice, neat package. It is our job to make a difference in the lives of others and to take care of people irrespective of borders. If someone is in need, it makes no difference where they are from or who they are, except to say they are human.

I have long said that we need to stop looking to politicians and start encouraging the work of missionaries and other individuals who are willing to make trips on missions to bring needed medical, dental, nutritional, hygienic, and yes, even spiritual matters to those in other lands who do not have the basics of what they need. A politician's work comes and goes, ending when their term in office is up. The work we are willing to do for those who are most in need is something that will never go away, not until Jesus comes back, because He wants to ensure we have the most opportunities to bring His active work to them, right where they are.

- DAILY DISCIPLINE: HONOR THE NEEDS THAT EXIST BY DOING SOMETHING TO HELP YOURSELF.

Advocating the Peace That Passes all Understanding

AND GOD'S PEACE, WHICH IS SO GREAT WE CANNOT UNDERSTAND IT
[TRANSCENDS/SURPASSES ALL COMPREHENSION], WILL KEEP [GUARD]
YOUR HEARTS AND MINDS IN CHRIST JESUS.
(PHILIPPIANS 4:7)

- DAILY READING: JOHN 14:1-31

I don't think it's terribly far-fetched to say that we live in an angry, angry world. Social media abounds with hot-headed people who just have to say one thing about social commentary, events, politics, or to target someone else. Road rage, something I'd never heard of until I was nearly an adult, is a very real thing when people grow angry and irate because someone else doesn't follow a traffic law, cuts them off in traffic, or is somehow perceived to be an inconsiderate driver to an angry person. Families live and dwell in seething anger as husbands and wives live with offenses committed one toward the other and siblings live with anger, hostility, favoritism, and rivalries throughout their lives. We see anger among employees and students who enter a workroom or classroom with guns and kill innocent lives. People live with hostility and resentment due to wrongs that have hurt them earlier in their lives, and a general sense that anger is going to transform the world – and not for the better – is the hush that most of us never speak of, even though we know that it's there.

Anger is a normal human emotion that stands as an alert system to us to let us know something is wrong. There's nothing wrong with being angry or feeling anger, but there is something wrong when anger takes over someone's entire life. If anger stops being a motivator to change or right wrong situations and rather becomes a way of living, a response to everything that happens, anger becomes a danger point.

The way we try to handle anger as a society is to make it go away or to try and explain the reasons why someone lives in a constant state of chronic anger. If we look over the years and years of anger management, it proves one consistent thing: anger, as we understand it, isn't going away, wishing it would disappear. We can't hope it'll go away if we understand enough about it and we can't try to get rid of our anger about things by doing other things.

To truly reach a place where we take our deep breaths and move in and out of our anger is to receive and advocate the peace that passes all understanding. Jesus promised it; thus it is a part of our walk as believers. With the world so angry and hostile, Jesus knew that the answer to find ourselves, to find contentment and satisfaction long-term and to see through to the truth of a better day was to walk in peace. If we receive the concept of peace that passes all understanding, something we can't fathom or imagine, that means we have adapted ourselves to receive something that is out of this world.

Yes, you will get angry. Yes, you will be angry at times. Yes, there is probably some part of you that, if you thought about it long enough, is angry about something, somewhere. By the end of this day, you will probably find something to be angry about. The antidote: receive and advocate the peace that passes understanding. In an angry world, the only lasting solution is peace.

- DAILY DISCIPLINE: SPEND TEN MINUTES IN QUIET MEDITATION ON THE PRINCIPLE OF PEACE.

- DAY 59 -

Colorful Restoration

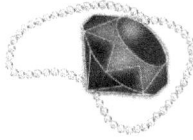

IF MY FATHER AND MOTHER LEAVE [ABANDON] ME,
THE LORD WILL TAKE ME IN.
(PSALM 27:10)

- DAILY READING: ISAIAH 49:14-18

One day a new college graduate "came out" to her parents. She had been struggling for a long time with her sexual identity as a lesbian and the frustration she experienced because she worried that her very conservative Christian family would not accept her if they knew. The reality was her fears of non-acceptance were very real. The very night she came out to her parents, she was thrown out of the house. In some ways, this young woman was lucky, because she had a great support system and people who she could live with temporarily until she found a job and proper housing. She had great spiritual support from leadership that loved her and others who cared about her. Unfortunately, too many lesbian, gay, bisexual, and transgender individuals (LGBTQ+) do not have this support.

LGBTQ+ issues are hot from pulpits and ministers who are itching to talk about sin and point such in the direction of the LGBTQ+ community. When they start up, they are, most often, likely to get a riled response from their congregants encouraging them forward. As a result, being classified as "gay," "bisexual," or "transgender" elicits a certain response from families, friends, and spiritual leaders who are unwilling to love or receive a person who experiences sexual or gender differences from what is perceived to be the "norm."

No matter how you feel about LGBTQ+, nobody should have to live with what much of the LGBTQ+ community encounters on a regular basis. 25% of homeless gay and lesbian teens become homeless the very day they come out to their parents. 40% of all homeless youth are gay or lesbian. 70% of these homeless LGBT youth commit suicide.

Gay and lesbian teens are two to three times more likely to commit suicide than other youths. About 30% of all suicides have been related to sexual identity crisis. Gay, lesbian, and transgender teens are five times more likely to miss school because of bullying or harassment. 15-43% of LGBTQ+ workers have been fired, denied promotions, or harassed. There are still twenty-eight states where an individual can be fired for being gay, and for no other reason.[16]

Looking into these statistics should show us there is a true mission field among the LGBTQ+ community where people need to feel the love of our God, Who created the rainbow as a sign of covenant with them as much as anyone else, hug and embrace them in a way that no human being can possibly ever do. Feeling failures, discrimination, dishonesty and lies from people who promise to do one thing but do another can leave any human being empty and needing to be filled with something eternal and spiritual, a promise that can never be lost, nor changed. Our pulpits are too often filled with hate against LGBT individuals, not letting them know that there is safety in God, safety in true spirituality, and a home for anyone who is ready and willing to lay their burdens, hurts and emptiness down to pick up eternal rest and promise in Him.

- DAILY DISCIPLINE: REACH OUT TO AN INDIVIDUAL YOU KNOW WHO IS LGBT WITH THE LOVE OF GOD AND THE CONSISTENCY OF SUPPORT.

- Day 60 -
Helping My Sister Heal

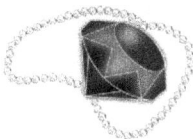

I will make you and the woman enemies to each other [place hostility/enmity between you and the woman]. Your descendants [seed] and her descendants [seed] will be enemies. One of her descendants [He] will crush your head, and you will bite [strike; bruise; crush] His heel [Rom. 16:20; Rev. 12:9]."
(Genesis 3:15)

- Daily Reading: Ruth 1:18-22

We hear a lot about Eve: the good, the bad, and the very bad. Most of it could fall in the "very bad" category. After all, Eve seemed to have it all: she had a man who was perfect, she never had to worry he was going to look at another woman or have an affair, and they lived in paradise. In keeping with what we know about Adam and Eve, Eve fell hard because she spent time listening to the devil. Together, Adam and Eve wanted more. They had it all, and it still wasn't enough because Satan planted a little bug that something else was out there. As a result, they pursued that thing unto death...all because they listened to the devil. We hear a lot about Eve's relationship to Adam as a result, and the consequences therein. If we aren't careful, we can begin to believe that only male/female relationships were affected by sin. If we believe that, we can also believe only male/female relationships find redemption in Christ.

One of the greatest consequences of sin is the division of God's women, one to another. We still haven't turned to crush the enemy's head...because we're too busy crushing one another. The serpent knows exactly what he is doing because he has transferred the hatred we are to have for him toward one another. We're too busy being jealous and envious to realize that if we step back, we all have that promise to crush the enemy, not each other. In Christ, God has given women a great promise that He did not give to men: He has placed enmity between us and the devil. Women, by nature, know how to fight the enemy because in the promise of enmity is the promise of the seed to come. It's spiritual and it's natural: it's the promise to carry and deliver the Word to come. But we are fighting the wrong enemy! My sister in Christ should not be my enemy, and I should not be hers. Rather, we should fight Satan together.

If we fight each other, we don't fight the enemy. When God first gave me the vision for women's ministry, it was to see the women of God healed, whole, restored, and working together, recognizing their call. It's not about fighting over men, trying to figure out who we should be to a man or what society wants us to be, but seeing who God has called us to be. We are here to stop the fighting over men, the cat calls, and competition one to another, and to just step up to the plate and say "Here I am, Lord." We're here for this transformation, this power, this empowerment that comes only through the Holy Spirit as we stand on our spiritual authority.

Pray for a woman of God that you know. Pray for her strength and her success. Ask God to bless her and shower over her life. Ask the Lord to heal your heart of animosity you may have toward your sister in the Lord. Let Him show you some way you can encourage a sister on today and do it. Be an encouragement, an agent of hope and help, and an inspiration. Help her to heal. Be a solution, not a complication, to her problems. Most of all, love your sister....and show her...and put on your best pair of demon-stomping shoes together and step on his head.

- DAILY DISCIPLINE: REACH OUT TO YOUR SISTER IN THE FAITH AND MAKE THE POINT TO SUPPORT HER THROUGH WHATEVER SHE IS GOING THROUGH RIGHT NOW IN HER LIFE.

- DAY 61 -
Voices to Challenge

THEN HE SAID, "TODAY I STAND AND DARE [DEFY; CHALLENGE]
THE ARMY [RANKS] OF ISRAEL! SEND ONE OF YOUR MEN [GIVE ME A MAN]
TO FIGHT ME!"
(1 SAMUEL 17:10)

- DAILY READING: 1 SAMUEL 17:1-49

When we were kids, one of the biggest things we all hated dealing with was bullying. If you were in any way smaller than normal, taller than normal, skinnier than normal, chubbier than normal, wore glasses, had different hair color or different style of hair, or had anything about you that was different, you were a target for a bully. Bullies liked to make sure they created fear in people and that you would do what they wanted because standing up to them was scary.

Bullying was bad enough when we were children. Losing our lunch money, our shoes, or getting hurt because of a fight or an attack ruined our days and sometimes our years if the bullying persisted. It was hard enough to face the day-after-day harassment of a bully without external threats that modern-day bullying has created. We didn't have to face the reality that our problems with a bully might wind up all over the internet or that parents or teachers involved in the situation wouldn't take it seriously.

Bullying has reached epidemic levels due to cyber bullying and people who use social media and the internet to harass others. On top of this issue, many parents and teachers alike do not take the issue of bullying seriously, so the problem continues without resolution. In the United States, there is no federal anti-bullying law. While all but one of the states have laws in place to prevent bullying, bullying is not considered illegal.[17] The line between harassment (which is illegal) and bullying (which is not illegal) is often fine, and most people do not press charges or take steps against a bully.

I'm not going to pretend that bullying doesn't happen to adults in our society, either. As an adult, I have been both cyber-harassed and cyber-bullied by people who felt the internet gave them the edge they needed to spread lies or intimidate me. Bullying is a pervasive problem in a world where people think they can get away with anything if there are no consequences and others are afraid to do something.

The solution to bullying is to become a voice that challenges it. The primary way bullying continues is through victimization that makes people so intimidated and afraid to speak up about it, they keep silent. They might fear someone else might think they are weak or they are falling into a victim's trap and looked down upon as "allowing" someone else to do this to them. Bullying is the problem and responsibility of the bully, and the only thing we do wrong when bullying starts is keep our thoughts to ourselves.

Children should be taught to speak up if they or someone they know is being bullied. They should know the right ways to get help and that adults in their life will take such matters seriously. Parents of bullies need to end the patterns of bullying now. All of us should speak up when someone is trying to intimidate or harass someone else. Bullying ends when we voice our challenge to the system.

- DAILY DISCIPLINE: STAND UP TO A BULLY.

- DAY 62 -
Embracing Different Viewpoints

WHEN YOU DO THINGS, DO NOT LET SELFISHNESS [RIVALRY; SELFISH
AMBITION] OR PRIDE BE YOUR GUIDE. INSTEAD, BE HUMBLE
AND GIVE MORE HONOR [REGARD; VALUE] TO OTHERS THAN TO YOURSELVES.
(PHILIPPIANS 2:3)

- DAILY READING: TITUS 3:9-11

When I was in junior high there was a girl in my class that I did not get along with, no matter what I did or how hard I tried. On the surface, we should have been friends. We both had strong personalities and many similar interests, including journalism, writing, theater, and a love for reading. No matter how much we had in common, it seemed like we had more things that made us opposites. The differences we had and the obvious disagreements we shared were a source of contention, causing arguments that were so notable, other students would gather around and watch us as we would debate. Standing toe-to-toe and as close as eye-to-eye as we could get (I was shorter, even back then), the debates would rage on until we had to go to class or until someone forced us to stop. We would get easily angry and embittered toward one another and made sure to avoid each other when it came time for group projects. Working together, talking, socializing, and doing anything productive was out of the question.

We had the excuse that we were still kids and still figuring out how to navigate ourselves, our tempers and our opinions with others back then. It disturbs me now, over twenty years later, to see adults behave with the same type of unrelenting attitudes when it comes to handling different viewpoints. Especially when it comes to matters of faith and politics, we have a hard time embracing people who feel differently than we do and coming to a place of understanding when we face disagreements.

Learning about others is one of the most important things we can do as human beings. If everyone in your life looks like you, sounds like you, and feels like you do, then you are doing something wrong. If we call ourselves social activists, individuals who care about and advocate for the rights of others, we can't advocate for those we do not know. All of us can say we support a cause but quickly change our tune when we are confronted with the realities and harshness of it up close. The key to being a good activist, someone who is interested in change and moving society forward, is to be someone who surrounds themselves with the diversity present in our world and the diversities present in life.

To do this, you must learn how to embrace different viewpoints. Embracing a viewpoint doesn't mean you readily accept it as your own or that you want to change your whole way of living and believing to align with what someone else believes. It means you can hold out your arms and embrace a person, no matter what they think or believe, and love them as they are, because they are human. It means that when you are confronted with an opposing viewpoint, you give it the respect it deserves and accept the points in your own beliefs that merit challenge and change. None of us has a perfect theory or viewpoint and learning to embrace and accept the fact that this world is full of different thoughts, feelings and opinions will launch us much further in our purpose if we step out and acknowledge they are there.

- DAILY DISCIPLINE: REFRAIN FROM ARGUING WHEN DIFFERENCES OF OPINION ARISE.

- DAY 63 -
Blessed are the Pure in Heart

THEY ARE BLESSED WHOSE THOUGHTS ARE PURE
[OR WHOSE HEARTS ARE PURE; THE PURE IN HEART], FOR THEY WILL SEE GOD.
(MATTHEW 5:8)

- DAILY READING: PSALM 51:10-17

Once upon a time, my former sorority held a conference at a church in South Carolina where the leader of that church was more than willing and eager to let us use her church for our event. She didn't even require we paid for use of the building, although the organization did offer to pay and did wind up giving her an offering. Once we were there, it was very evident she had a problem with our presence. The encounters with her were snide and rude, even though no one did or said anything to illicit such a response. The weekend ended when we showed up for a scheduled event and no one was sent to unlock the church. Our sorority host did not hear from her until a few days after the event was over to tell her that "maybe it all worked out for the best."

On the surface, her offer seemed like a good thing, a viable answer to our situation. It sounded like someone was stepping up to meet an existing need and do something good for the organization and those within the organization that this woman knew. There was nothing on the surface to suggest a need for caution, but the truth is that the woman's motives were done in such a way that were not "pure in heart."

As human beings, we are quick to associate people's motives with the outcome or result of whatever they are doing. If someone comes along and is rude or nasty to us from the get-go, we assume that person has a bad motive and is someone we should stay away from. There is some truth to this, and it is something to aware ourselves of and keep in mind. The problem with this, however, is that we spend so much time running from people who are upfront about their motives that we miss the reality that others might have ulterior motives, ideas stemming from realities found deep in the impurities of the heart.

Purity in the heart reveals our motives, which are the thoughts and intents behind our actions. The secret to right motives is to be what the Bible calls "pure in heart." If you are pure in heart, it means your motives, actions, and purposes are right before God. You aren't doing things to be seen of men, to have earthly successes, or to try and get to someone else through motives of power or control. The purity – without spot or wrinkle, completely honorable and perfect in the sight of God – renders right actions and right spirituality.

Those who are pure in heart shall see God. That is their reward because they have been purified and perfected enough, tried and still standing, to see God as He is, without veil or blockage between them. The revelation of God is theirs because they have taken His nature upon themselves. Before you go thinking "at least I am not as bad as so-and-so," back up for a minute. None of us are there all the way, just yet, but we can all start and work on ourselves and our own motives in the meantime. Set your sights on doing as God would do and loving as God loves, because that will change your heart.

- DAILY DISCIPLINE: REPENT FROM THOSE THINGS YOU DO THAT ARE NOT "PURE IN HEART."

- DAY 64 -
Christian Feminists Changed the World

HOW LONG WILT THOU GO ABOUT, O THOU BACKSLIDING DAUGHTER?
FOR THE LORD HATH CREATED A NEW THING IN THE EARTH,
A WOMAN SHALL COMPASS A MAN.
(JEREMIAH 31:22, KJV)

- DAILY READING: GALATIANS 3:26-29

*I*f you have been led to believe that feminism is incompatible with Christianity, think again. The truth about feminism and the feminist movement, all the way back to its inception, is that it has always had Christian roots. The first feminists in American history were Christian women who believed in the fundamental equality of women and men and desired to study in seminary, hold ordination credentials, maintain their own property, vote, and receive equal pay for their jobs. They fought, labored, established their own schools and seminaries, maintained their own newspapers and information, and lived with the harassment of regular members of society. Early feminists faced jail time, imprisonment, social isolation, discrimination, items thrown at them, police brutality, and general mistreatment because they stood for something that others were unwilling to stand for.

Feminist understanding has now spread to secular as well as Christian understanding and is understood to mean different things to different women but overall stands for the same beliefs and principles that men and women are equal and women deserve equality within society. It also means this groundbreaking, society-shaking ideal still threatens much of the world, even now. Feminists today still face social discrimination, isolation, police brutality, and general mistreatment because the principle that men and women are equal is still one not acknowledged by most cultures. In some parts of the world, feminists still face imprisonment or social attack from authorities because the concept is still so revolutionary.

In many churches, classifying oneself as a "feminist" is often considered a threatening or anti-Christian sentiment. Many churches desire to adopt a traditional exterior and understanding of family values and find the idea that women desire to be treated as equals, as equal partners in marriage, own their own property, maintain jobs, or work in ministry as threatening notions to traditional ideals. Much of what we see in American Christianity represents patriarchal ideals and American church structure reflects more of a colonial landowner or head of household than true church structure we see present in the five-fold ministry. In an effort to maintain a cultural identity, American churches are ignoring the needs of their women and failing to uphold their esteem as people.

Whether you are a man or a woman, if you believe that men and women are equal, that they should be paid the same amount of money to do the same job, that women should have access to healthcare services and that it is not the government's job to make decisions for them, that women and girls should have the opportunity to decide what they want to do with their lives and should have access to education, then surprise…you might not have ever guessed it, but you are a feminist! Embrace your history and realize the ground that others have tread on this path to equality.

- DAILY DISCIPLINE: RESEARCH A WOMAN IN CHRISTIAN HISTORY WHO CHANGED THE WORLD.

- Day 65 -

Visiting Those in Prison

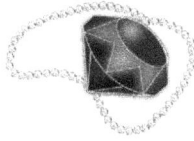

I WAS…IN PRISON, AND YOU DID NOT CARE FOR [VISIT; LOOK AFTER] ME.
(MATTHEW 25:43)

- DAILY READING: ACTS 12:1-19

I'd done education in prison, I had done training in prison, I had prayed for people in prison, but I had never formally visited an inmate until one day, a few years ago, when I made the trek up to Lawrenceville, Virginia to visit an inmate I was training and covering at the time. The trip took me more than three hours in the car due to several detours and by the time I got to the prison, I was not only hot and tired, I was definitely not in the mood to deal with snobbish, out-of-sorts guards who picked at my attire (I was wearing cleric's civic attire), who couldn't find me on the visitor's list, and who made me wait a ridiculous length of time before I was able to see the inmate I was there to visit. By the time I left and made it home, I was exhausted and frustrated, because I felt as if the system had done everything possible to ruin my day.

What made me stop and think after the fact was what families of inmates must go through to see their loved ones, especially if they live far away or are travelling with children. The practical hardship of visiting an inmate on a regular basis exists, especially given it is very possible to travel all the way to the prison to see the person and the jail either closes visitor hours early or you are unable to get in through the prison during visitor hours. Then there is the additional expense of buying food or other items inside the jail that charges sometimes more than 500% the cost of what those same items would be on the outside.

Visiting someone in prison is not a fun experience. While you are a visitor in jail, you are treated as if you are an inmate yourself by staff who tend to be abrupt and intolerant. You spend a lot of time waiting and sometimes that waiting will not have many results. It sounds like a long and time-wasting process, so the question remains: why does God tell us to visit those in prison?

It's not a big secret that when someone goes to prison, they don't tend to get a lot of visitors. Family and friends can only come so often, and many stop making the effort to visit an inmate. More than this, the social isolation of inmate life means inmates forget about the relevance of human interaction and proper ways to interact with other people. Since many inmates do eventually get out of prison, it is important they remember how to talk, interact, and behave with others on the outside.

More than this, all of us experience the feeling of being locked away, hidden, or kept from something because something else is keeping us bound. We've all been in situations where we feel trapped, like we can't get out and someone or something else is holding our future. Maybe we've even been in those situations because of things we have done ourselves or things that happened because we were in the wrong place at the wrong time with the wrong people. No matter how we got there, we know what a difficult and unpleasant experience it can be to feel trapped and unable to get away. God expects us to look upon such situations with compassion, recognizing that if we reach out, forgiveness becomes an accessible, powerful freedom available to others.

- DAILY DISCIPLINE: INTERVIEW A FORMER INMATE ABOUT THE PRISON EXPERIENCE AND ABOUT THE RELEVANCE IN VISITS TO INMATES.

- DAY 66 -
Forming a United Front

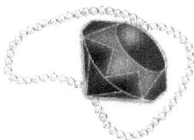

MAKE EVERY EFFORT TO PRESERVE THE UNITY OF [PROVIDED BY; AVAILABLE THROUGH] THE SPIRIT IN [THROUGH] THE PEACE THAT JOINS US TOGETHER [BOND OF PEACE].
(EPHESIANS 4:3)

- DAILY READING: PSALM 133:1-3

Working well with others is one of the hardest things we are faced with this side of heaven. Some might think that to be an odd statement, especially given many of the difficulties we are faced with in this life. If you think about those difficulties we face, what is the root of their difficulty? Most likely, the difficulty comes when it is time to do something or work with someone who either doesn't have the same heart for the issue or you are unable to work with someone else due to something they have done. We can probably think of several projects or assignments offhand that went awry because we had to deal with someone who was just too difficult to work with. That having been said, it's easy to sit around and bemuse all the reasons why working with someone else is impossible. We all can think of someone who gets under our skin and rubs us the wrong way. Yet have we ever considered how easy or difficult we make the prospect of working with us?

I never promised that talking about a united front would be easy! To bring ourselves to the point where we can work with others and consider the cause we work as primary, we need to be aware of the things that make us tick and how easy or difficult we are to work with. We can point fingers at everyone else's issues with unity, but if we are just as hostile and belligerent, we are a part of the unity problem. Unity is something we must do on purpose. We can't achieve unity by sitting on the sidelines and waiting for everyone else to fix themselves. We must be willing to get in our own time, our own assessments of self, and see just how committed we are to our cause in order to participate in that united work.

United fronts start with unity, and they end with a show of force. When I say "force," I don't mean violence or weaponry. I mean a deliberate, on purpose effort to bring about whatever change needs to come into existence. Making that effort means we must know what we advocate, knowing it forward and backward, and brainstorming all the different ways that bringing that issue into the focus can effectively render the attention the issue needs. It takes focus and discipline, purpose and long-term commitment. We need to all agree to stick with whatever we need to as long as it takes, not distancing nor dropping the issue if it gets hard.

In the middle, smack dab between unity and force, we find formation. If we are to be taken seriously, we need to fall into a proper setup that will most effectively use the gifts and skills that each of us has. That's where recognizing ourselves and our issues comes into play. We can't do what we aren't suited to do, and if we find ourselves trying to outdo everyone else, we are not going to do what we are best suited to do. Yes, in unity, we all find our place. We put together all of us, in ways that we are most effective, and we bring our issue or issues to the world with passion and purpose. There's no greater way to do something and show that people can work together.

- DAILY DISCIPLINE: RECONCILE WITH ANOTHER TOWARD GREATER UNITY.

- DAY 67 -
Respecting Unjust Authority

THEN JESUS SAID TO THEM, "GIVE [RENDER] TO CAESAR THE THINGS
THAT ARE CAESAR'S, AND GIVE TO GOD THE THINGS THAT ARE GOD'S."
(MATTHEW 22:21)

- DAILY READING: ROMANS 13:1-7

When we start talking about government leaders or even authority in general from a Biblical perspective, it's pretty typical to find a variety of opinions. Some feel what the Bible has to say about authority is obsolete and should be disregarded. Some think we must take the Bible's words about authority literally and should do so with no deviation or consideration. Some think the Bible's words on authority can only qualify if a leader is Christian. Some think the Bible's words about governing powers are conditional on the heart or situation in which a leader finds themselves. Still, there are others who have totally different viewpoints on authority from a Biblical perspective. The reason there is no one singular perspective is because of the question, what do we do when a ruling leader is unjust? Surely, we don't have one definition of "unjust," either. What may seem like a perfectly fair rule to one person probably doesn't seem that way to someone else. Thus, the question comes into play – how do we handle unjust authority?

I believe the Bible speaks as it does on authority because being a leader is a hard job, no matter what sector (spiritual, governmental, employment, etc.) one may govern. It's difficult because dealing with large groups of people means someone is always unhappy, someone else thinks they could do the job better, and someone always has a complaint. It's difficult having to balance the thoughts of the individual welfare along with group welfare, and God wanted us to consider these things when we start dealing with authority that is unjust. I do not believe God ever intended for people to be mistreated or to remain mute when their rights were violated, but at the same time, God wanted us to realize there are certain ways to do things that are more effective than others. If we have a point to get across, it goes a lot further if we are respectful of authority that exists than if we try to do things in pure rebellion.

The Bible's teaching on authority exists to remind us that the concepts of order and authority both come from God. It doesn't mean every leader in history (or even modern times) has exercised authority in a godly way. It doesn't mean every leader is godly, but that governmental authority and functioning is godly, and there is nothing wrong with a leader assuming an office or making a decision as a part of that process. Exerting authority is not wrong, but misusing authority certainly is.

If we want to advance our causes and beliefs, we are going to have to find the balance within ourselves, of respect for ungodly authority. We don't have to like our leaders, but we do need to lift them up in prayer and remember that our presentation of ourselves speaks far more than any improper conduct can. We must remember that their office is there, whether we like it or not, and that we are here, established to transform the world through love and respect rather than embitterment and further hate. Hating a leader won't bring change. Showing honor will; not all at once, but one step at a time.

- DAILY DISCIPLINE: PRAY FOR THE GRACE TO RESPECT UNJUST LEADERSHIP.

- DAY 68 -
Shut Up and Do Something...

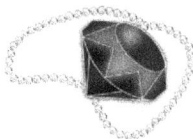

...BECAUSE THE KINGDOM OF GOD IS PRESENT [OR CONSISTS] NOT IN TALK BUT IN POWER.
(1 CORINTHIANS 4:20)

- DAILY READING: JAMES 14:22-26

Once upon a time I would get so excited about the idea of a conference or a project that I would have to go online or call up several friends and talk about whatever it was that demanded my attention at the time. I'd be all bubbly and up, pepped up to say, "God showed me this and we are going to do it!" I didn't stop and pause to pray or consider how much work or money something was going to take to see fruition. I ran my mouth, thinking that talking about the idea was going to take care of the work involved in it. Now, in hindsight, I am shocked to think about the number of plans and projects I got so caught up in talking about, I never made a reality.

My behavior reflected the mistakes that are all-too-commonly seen among those with a vision today. We are so excited about the ideas we have, we forget those ideas don't work without practical action. We want to express what is important to us and we hope if we talk about it, it'll make others want to get involved, too. Instead, we find a graveyard of ideas and concepts that fell by the wayside because we never turned those ideas or thoughts into actions.

Think for a few minutes about all the plans, ideas, and visions you have shared that have never come to pass. As Americans, we love to talk. We love talk shows, talk radio, telephones, video conferencing, webcams, and any other means available to try and verbally communicate with others. We love to complain about whatever is wrong and bemoan when we feel we've been wronged by someone or something. We've even taken to talking about talking in church. From gossip to declarations, to decreeing and declaring, we believe speaking is the secret to doing all sorts of things in the spiritual realm.

No question at all, talking is important. It is one of the primary ways we interact with other human beings. Being able to convey thoughts, feelings, wants, and ideas is necessary for our survival in this world. We need to have a means to do this, and talk is God's answer to these essential communication needs. There's nothing wrong with talking or speech…as long as it's not all that we do. Unfortunately, we've been taught that words have power for so long, we've forgotten that actions have power, too. We need to make sure our actions speak louder than our words. God has not created us to be people who do nothing more than talk. He has created us with the ability to speak so we can put our ideas together and start doing those things. Speech has never been a substitution for action, but a catalyst to bring about the challenges and changes of life.

Sometimes it would behoove us to stop talking so much and get ourselves to work on action. We can spend our entire lives in meetings, phone calls, and gab sessions to try and rally support, or we can just do whatever we are looking to do and start connecting with others who have similar ideals and concepts. Never forget they say "talk is cheap" for a reason – it doesn't mean we'll ever do what we say.

- DAILY DISCIPLINE: THAT PROMISE YOU MADE TO DO SOMETHING? DO IT!

- DAY 69 -
Compassionate Care

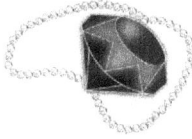

My dear friend [Beloved], I pray that you are doing well [prospering] in every way [all respects] and that your health is good, just as your soul is doing fine [it is well with your soul; your soul is prospering].
(3 John 2)

- DAILY READING: MARK 5:21-42

At current, approximately 39.9 million people live with HIV worldwide.[18] Over 630,000 people died from HIV in 2023.[19] This sobering reality should be enough to make all of us take notice of the disease and realize that even though we don't hear about it in the news every day, HIV has not gone anywhere and is still a serious illness that merits our notice and attention.

HIV is an acronym for Human Immunodeficiency Virus, the illness and virus that causes AIDS (Acquired Immune Deficiency Syndrome), late-stage HIV. Despite research efforts and attempts to find a cure, HIV remains incurable. There are extensive treatments for HIV that help patients live longer lives, but HIV is still a disease with no cure and serious health implications. HIV is transmitted between people through direct blood contact, sexual contact (oral, anal, or vaginal sex), breastmilk, pregnancy, sharing drug needles or paraphernalia, or an infected blood transfusion. HIV does not spread with nominal contact, from hugging or kissing someone, bug bites, sharing cups, spoons, or utensils, talking to a person or caring about them. HIV is not now, nor has ever been, a "gay disease." People of all sexual orientations, religions, nationalities, and cultures have been infected with HIV. The advice on how to avoid HIV infection remains the same: use barrier-protection (condoms) when sexually involved with another person or avoid sexual contact with someone who is infected; do not share drug needles or drug paraphernalia; avoid direct blood contact; don't share personal items (razors, toothbrushes) and don't get a homemade or prison tattoo.[20] Despite these facts, we still see many people who stereotype HIV, who stigmatize HIV patients, and who don't think they can get HIV because they don't fall into a certain sexual orientation or social demographic.

It's easy to look at an HIV or AIDS patient and think they "deserve" to be sick because of something they are perceived to have done, or to step back and divide infected patients into the categories of "deserving" the disease or having it "through no fault of their own." Nobody asks to have HIV. It is not a divine punishment for sin, because if it were, we would all have it. We are all sinners and most, if not all, of us have done things that should have landed us in far worse shape than we are in today. None of us has the right to judge someone's life based on a diagnosis.

HIV patients deal with stigma, isolation, loss of family and friends, fear and panic, and a general sense that life, as they know it, will never be the same again. If we claim to believe in healing, in wholeness, and in love, we must stand as agents of compassion and hope in a world that echoes stereotype and darkness. I call it "Compassionate Care" because in compassion, we never judge, and in care, we offer just what is needed at just the right time.

- DAILY DISCIPLINE: GET TESTED FOR HIV TO EXPERIENCE WHAT THE PROCESS IS LIKE FOR PATIENTS.

- DAY 70 -
Providing for Those Who Grieve

HE HAS SENT ME TO COMFORT ALL THOSE WHO ARE SAD [MOURN]
AND TO HELP THE SORROWING [MOURNING] PEOPLE OF JERUSALEM
[ZION; LOCATION OF THE TEMPLE; 59:20].
(ISAIAH 61:3)

- DAILY READING: PSALM 34:15-22

Before the late 1960s, grief was not something most medical health specialists took into account when assessing an individual's mental state. This all changed with the work of Elisabeth Kubler-Ross, a psychiatrist who pioneered exploration into the world of grief for professionals all over the world. Her book, *On Death and Dying*, was the first look many gave into the process of death, near death, and for those who experience severe and intense loss in their lives. As a part of her work, she taught on different stages of grief, which may occur in any order: denial, anger, bargaining, depression, and acceptance. Even though the original book spoke about death and the experience many have surrounding death, her work also includes application for any type of major or serious loss in life, including those who lose someone in death, the loss of a job, divorce, or even chronic illness.[21]

Grief tends to be an uncomfortable topic for many. We don't like to think of the hurts and offenses of life as taking a long-term toll, which is exactly what grief is. Grief is the persistent state of sadness because of severe loss, hurt, or offense, often dealt through some of life's harshest and most unpleasant blows. When confronted with loss or something so severe that it is life altering and hard to accept, people experience different stages of the grieving process and go through any number of measures to come to acceptance. Unfortunately, many never find the acceptance they need to move forward and come to a place where healing is possible.

When God tells us about providing for those who grieve, He isn't just talking about handing someone a Bible and telling them that everything is going to be all right. In ancient times, grieving was done for specified periods of time. During those interims, the grieving were to do nothing but grieve. They did not change or wash their clothes, they did not bathe, they did not cook, and sometimes they did not eat. They did nothing but focus on their sorrow and sadness, in efforts to devote themselves fully to that process. It was believed that by doing so, moving on with life would be, in the long run, easier. This meant the grieving needed provision – care, food, clothing, attention, and assistance – to do what they were unable to do for themselves.

Providing for those who grieve is about developing a deep relationship with someone to be a catalyst for their needed healing, helping them as they progress between different stages, and letting them know someone is there for them, no matter how dark or difficult the experience may become. Grief is one of those things that people often experience alone, especially when things grow too heavy or intense for others who can move forward more easily. The longer you are there – a friend, offering food or help, a listening ear, and the support needed – the easier the process to finding hope and life once again.

- DAILY DISCIPLINE: PROVIDE FOOD OR ANOTHER NEED TO SOMEONE WHO IS GRIEVING.

- DAY 71 -
The Social Call of the Teacher: Education

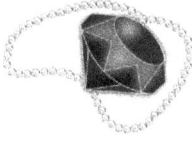

TEACH [GIVE TO] THE WISE, AND THEY WILL BECOME EVEN WISER;
TEACH [INFORM] GOOD PEOPLE [THE RIGHTEOUS], AND THEY WILL LEARN
EVEN MORE [ADD TO THEIR LEARNING].
(PROVERBS 9:9)

- DAILY READING: PSALM 32:8-11

Education may seem like an odd priority to the church, especially considering that through much of church history, the majority of church members were illiterate and largely uneducated. In fact, if we look through many dark periods of church history, it appears institutionalized religious movements desired church people to remain in darkness and ignorance. Many find it unfathomable to believe that, at one point in time, it was illegal for a layperson to read the Bible. At the same time, it was also thanks to the influence of the church and the work of the church that many different scientific, intellectual, and educational achievements were made throughout history.

We can't embrace the work of the church without embracing the work of education because the way we come to a greater understanding of God and what He wants us to learn as people only comes to pass through educated means. That is one of the primary reasons we have teachers within the ranks of the five-fold ministry. God knew that as a part of His new creation, present within the church, we would need to be educated and re-educated within our understanding of church and purpose. To be properly educated (as He desires us to be) we need guidance, found within the gift of those who teach the church.

Western culture has created an elitist faith when we believe all we need to do is read the Bible and we can all figure out the exact same conclusions of truth for ourselves. It is elitist because to read the Bible, one must first know how to read. To know how to read means that one has been taught, and has achieved a certain level of education in one's life. While we sit in the west and argue over what different Bible verses mean or how different passages of the Bible should read, there is someone in the world who has had no chance of any education because there has never been a social revolution within their nations to push for the education of their students.

757 million adults worldwide do not have basic reading and writing skills. Two-thirds of these adults are women. In sub-Saharan Africa, one out of three young women cannot read. More than half of children who are out of school are girls. Worldwide, 780 million adults and 103 million young people (15-24) are illiterate.[22] If we look at history, it was the work of tireless missionaries who went into areas that were often dangerous, inhospitable and tiresome to work among native populations and bring forth reading, writing, and basic educational value along with spiritual education.

If we believe that God cares about us in our entirety, then God cares about our levels of education. I'd go as far to say that He expects us, as Christians, to stand behind solid educators and cheer on the teachers of the church, no matter how they are specifically called to teach and flow in their spiritual gift. Imagine a church where no one can read or write – and then thank a teacher for making sure you can.

- DAILY DISCIPLINE: READ AN EDUCATIONAL BOOK.

- DAY 72 -

Do not Pollute the Land Where You are

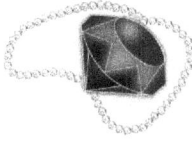

THE PEOPLE OF THE WORLD [NATIONS; GENTILES] WERE ANGRY [PS. 2:1],
BUT YOUR ANGER [WRATH] HAS COME. THE TIME HAS COME TO JUDGE
THE DEAD [DAN. 12:2], AND TO REWARD YOUR SERVANTS THE PROPHETS
AND YOUR HOLY PEOPLE [SAINTS], ALL WHO RESPECT YOU [THOSE WHO FEAR
YOUR NAME], SMALL AND GREAT. THE TIME HAS COME TO DESTROY THOSE
WHO DESTROY THE EARTH!
(REVELATION 11:18)

- DAILY READING: NUMBERS 35:33-34

When I discovered that a large summer camp owned by a Christian organization was one of the worst polluters of an upstate New York lake, I was instantly uninterested in whatever message about God they might feel compelled to share with me. The reason I was uninterested is because if they, as an organization, could not find it within themselves to uphold some respect for creation, how were they going to talk to me about respect for the One Who created it? When I state my thoughts like this, it probably makes perfect sense to those who are reading it, but would you be surprised to learn that I have met several other Christians who displayed attitudes like those of the Christian organization mentioned above about creation?

I understand matters of ecology have become largely politicized and many Christians feel the government infringes on their own personal rights when it comes to matters of pollution and environmental regulations. At the same time, we should all realize, the government would not have to intervene if we were willing to stand as good stewards with earthly resources and handle ourselves properly, exercising self-control and refraining from gluttony with existing natural resources. No matter what you feel about global warming, there is no denial we can have that needless pollution is wrong, as is destruction of the environment.

In early Biblical times, the main pollutant came from human blood and bodily fluids. They hadn't invented mass chemicals or things to destroy the environment yet. A mass number of chemicals released into the atmosphere damage air quality, cause allergies and asthma, and destroy the water and physical landmass in which we live. Over 100 million people die from pollution. Over 1 million seabirds and 100,000 sea mammals are killed by pollution every year. People who live in areas with high levels of air pollution are 20% more likely to die from lung cancer.[23] Clearly, no matter what someone might think about the politics of ecology, living in a world where we are poor stewards with what God has given to us has complications far and wide for all of us.

What can you do? It's not as bleak as it might seem. What you do can make a difference because stewardship always makes a difference. The advice and ideas aren't new, but it amazes me how many people still do not follow through to do them. Recycle your used plastic, paper, and glass items. In some areas, you can even recycle Styrofoam. Recycle cardboard. Endorse and support ecologically friendly ("green") companies instead of thinking they are just a marketing gimmick. Bring back the fine art of walking when it's possible and take an interest in biking or public transportation when it's available. Start or join a carpool to get to work. Participate in volunteer clean-up efforts when they are required. Spend some time in nature. Appreciate the beauty that God has created...and see God present within it.

- DAILY DISCIPLINE: RECYCLE!

- DAY 73 -
Change the World – Cross the Street

LET EACH OF US PLEASE OUR NEIGHBORS FOR THEIR GOOD,
TO HELP THEM BE STRONGER IN FAITH [EDIFY THEM; BUILD THEM UP].
(ROMANS 15:2)

- DAILY READING: LUKE 6:30-36

Whenever I think of the Hillsong United song, *Oceans*, God brings my attention to the line in the song, "Spirit lead me where my trust is without borders, Let me walk upon the waters, Wherever You would call me."[23] In hearing the words, and hearing the concepts, I have a moment of incredible clarity: when people sing this song, and sing that line, they feel all emotional and super-spiritual. In that state, feeling all…whatever…they are singing that line and have no idea what they are asking of God.

I never thought I'd see the day when half the internet would believe they were "called to the nations." Every time I scroll down my feed, I see at least two references to people pronouncing themselves "called to the nations." They can't expound on which nations they are called to, or what they are going to do when they get to "the nations," or how they are working on communicating with people once they get to "the nations" since they can barely speak English, but they insist they are called…elsewhere. Yet these are the same people who can't even walk across the street and help someone there…or walk down their street and reach out to someone in need…or drive themselves across town and visit a different church. Some have seen nothing but the inside of a pulpit for years and can't relate to the needs people have on a large scale, seeing there is a hurting world out there that needs Jesus.

When we ask the Spirit to lead us to a place where our trust is without borders, that means we are asking the Spirit to take us beyond what is comfortable for us. We are asking to cross the lines that society, our churches, our denominations, our families, and our own minds have established. We are asking that our call may take us wherever God wills it to go, wherever we are led. Walking upon the waters is about more than just literally walking on water - it is believing that no matter where God calls you, He will take you there and carry you back.

Being "called to the nations" sounds awesome, but that call to walk on water wherever He calls starts in a different way. Nobody is impressed with how far and how aggrandized you see your call. You want to see people impressed? Cross borders wherever you are. Go across the street, go next door, go down or up the street, go across your city, go across the country, go visit someone somewhere else. Prove you aren't afraid to cross the borders created by men. If you can't go across town, there is no way you can go across "borders" somewhere else. After all, the "nations" are all divided by borders that you can't be afraid to cross because some man put them there. If you want to be someone of change, that change starts with a willingness to go wherever God sends, whether it sounds glamorous in a Facebook status, or not.

Make change in someone's life. Make a difference for someone you know. Don't wait for big assignments to make a difference; never overlook the value of crossing your street.

- DAILY DISCIPLINE: FIND OUT ABOUT AN EVENT OR PROJECT AT A LOCAL CHURCH (OTHER THAN YOUR OWN) AND VISIT IT IN SUPPORT OF THAT MINISTRY'S WORK.

- DAY 74 -
Are You a Sheep or a Goat?

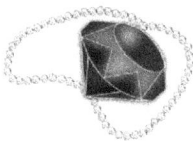

ALL THE NATIONS OF THE WORLD WILL BE GATHERED BEFORE HIM,
AND HE WILL SEPARATE THEM INTO TWO GROUPS [ONE FROM ANOTHER]
AS A SHEPHERD SEPARATES THE SHEEP FROM THE GOATS.
(MATTHEW 25:32)

- DAILY READING: MATTHEW 25:1-13

Have you ever wondered why the Bible mentions sheep and goats when it talks about the final judgment? If you study passages that relate to end times judgment, we aren't just compared to sheep and goats. We are also compared to wheat and tares, wise and foolish virgins, and people invited to a banquet who either show up or don't show up. Sheep and goats might be our favorite comparison, but the truth of all these different comparisons is the same basic message: As people, we will find ourselves in one of two categories. It should be our goal to be in one category rather than the other. The way we are in that group is to choose accordingly and make sure our actions match the faith we claim to have. We don't get to just be in one category because of what we believe.

Ouch. There's a message you won't hear preached often, but it is true, nonetheless. When it comes to being called wise or foolish, sheep or goat, wheat or tare, or showing up or staying home, the difference is how we live our faith. Those in the other category know, and don't do. Thus, we don't want to ever be people who know what we should do but choose not to do it.

In talking about our specifications for this devotion, I wanted to look up some of the natural differences between sheep and goats. There are some obvious differences in their statures and their diets, but the difference between a sheep or a goat lies in their nature and in the way that they live. Goats like to go their own way while sheep prefer the companionship of their flock, and goats live wild while sheep live in domestication.[24] This major difference explains to us the fundamental difference between sheep and goats and why they are used as such a powerful illustration of living faith and dead faith. If you are on the right side of things, you will prefer the companionship and spiritual placement you find in Christ, and you will not find yourself living wild or seeking to be off and wild, disobedient to what Christ commands. You will live content, ready to make a difference, ready to live right and do right in all situations.

Sometimes I think we make these things that pertain to faith much harder than they must be. We want to sit and dissect the Scriptures and take obedience out of the equation of our faith. We are still commanded to live and do right, and part of doing right requires us to do right by others. Every one of us is called to make that difference, do that one thing that will change someone's life and make God real to them constructively. Any one of us can talk about the goodness of God, as if it's an exclusive, intangible thing. All of us are commanded to make that goodness of God real to someone else.

In the end, you'll either be an old sheep or an old goat. Choose wisely.

- DAILY DISCIPLINE: LOOK UNTO THE SHEPHERD OF YOUR SOUL TO BECOME A BETTER SHEEP.

- DAY 75 -
Beauty for Ashes

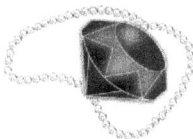

I WILL GIVE THEM A CROWN [GARLAND; HEADDRESS]
TO REPLACE THEIR ASHES...
(ISAIAH 61:3)

- DAILY READING: 1 JOHN 3:13-24

I've always loved plants and flowers. When I was younger, we had a wood stove, and we would save the ashes from one winter and use them to scatter and plant seeds the following year. Ashes always generate bigger, better, and healthier flowers than using regular dirt or soil. From the ashes of the winter there was incredible beauty discovered in the spring and summer. Winter, being a season of silence and often perceived to be a season of death, ushered in cold and a need for heat, and in that lack of natural warmth there was a promise of the future warmth and color of seasons to come. It required creativity and insight, but in every bucket of ashes was the promise of beautiful summer flowers to come.

In most cultures, ashes signify death. Cremation is a common treatment of dead bodies complete with funeral rites and ceremonies where the ashes are scattered. Bodies are also burned during times of pandemics, such as during the Black Plague. They signify all that is left of human life once it's over, the dust that we are prophesied to return unto when all our accomplishments mean nothing but in the memories of those who remember us. Ashes are an end, a finish, a completion...a reduction, if you will, to nothing.

It's amazing how many people live in a perpetual state of ashes, feeling as if life has no meaning and as if they are reduced to former memories that are no longer living or real. They are not physically dead, but live in a state of living death, stunted and stopped by an incident or a series of moments that changed their outlook on life.

To give beauty for ashes is something deeper than a women's conference theme or an idea for a sermon. It's about more than an opportunity to wear a flowered print dress or a big hat, or an excuse to give out flowers at church. Giving beauty for ashes literally means we take a situation that seems dead, a person that has a life that seems dead and lost, and we bring it back to life again with something powerful and beautiful. In exchanging beauty for ashes, we are exchanging death for life.

In every restored life, one that has passed from life to death and then to life again, we see a type of the resurrection. Every individual who experiences a powerful spiritual death reduces themselves to ashes, forever changed in form and in shape. They're reduced to nothingness, to a place where they are one with the experience of the dust of creation and of the true futility we can find in life. Sin causes us to lose; some more than others, all eventually in the same form of death. Finding beauty in loss – in spiritual death – in being reduced to nothing – enables one to rise again, to do the impossible and take one's identity back, as it has now been found in purpose wrapped up in the cross of Christ. Without Him, none of us have hope. With Him, all of us have hope to triumph again and make something beautiful out of something that ordinarily would look dead but now has life.

- DAILY DISCIPLINE: EITHER BUY OR GROW A PLANT FROM SEEDS AND WATCH THE PROCESS OF CARING AND TENDING TO IT.

- DAY 76 -

Loving Others as We Love Ourselves

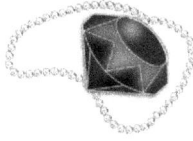

ONE MUST LOVE GOD WITH ALL HIS HEART, ALL HIS MIND, AND ALL HIS
STRENGTH. AND ONE MUST LOVE HIS NEIGHBOR AS HE LOVES HIMSELF.
THESE COMMANDS ARE MORE IMPORTANT THAN ALL THE ANIMALS
[BURNT OFFERINGS] AND SACRIFICES WE OFFER TO GOD
[1 SAM. 15:22; HOS. 6:6; MIC. 6:6–8].
(MARK 12:33)

• DAILY READING: LUKE 10:25-37

Every one of us has met someone we just didn't take well to and, well...just couldn't stand. We want them to go away as quickly as they appear and never have to deal with them again. It's easy for us to admit that loving someone like this is a challenge for us, but what about loving others who are close to us and who love us? Most of us would be quick to jump on the bandwagon and say how easy it is to love others who love us and what a blessing it is to have people who love us in our lives, and that we want others to have the best, wanting them to have everything they want, all the time.

It's easy to divide people into the love/hard to love category, but the truth about loving others is that it is typically not as simple as we would like to believe. Life throws us many curve balls and people tend to be confusing and inconsistent, so what do we do when that happens? What happens when the people who love us stop loving us, or we discover never really loved us to begin with? What do we do when we feel like our mutual love has been an exclusive love, hard to experience and totally wasted?

When the Bible tells us to love others as we would love ourselves, it's a lot harder of an aspiration to achieve than we might think at first glance. We are commanded to love others as ourselves, which means we love and consider ourselves and our needs. God doesn't call us to be so self-sacrificing that we forget about our interests, but too often, the concept of loving others in the same way as we love ourselves causes us to hit a complicated and worldly wall. It's not always easy to love ourselves, let alone other people, and when it comes to considering the concept of loving others, we are all quick to think it's a great idea, but how do we live it?

The Bible's teaching on loving others – all others – as ourselves is very revolutionary in and of itself. It forces us to go beyond the concepts of familial or national loyalty and challenges us to care about people beyond cross borders and natural lines of thinking. We are commanded to love others as we love ourselves, no matter who they are. The command itself manifests as we want the same for others, that best, that truly central truth and goodness, as we would want for ourselves. No longer do we place ourselves or those who love us as much as we love them back in the primary seat in our lives; instead, we want the same for everyone, esteeming no one higher than we esteem any other.

This is a high and hard principle to live in one's life, because human nature demands a certain level of partiality on our part. We do favors for those who can advance us; we help those first who want to help us back; we like those who are good to us and who treat us like we feel we should be treated. It's hard to desire the best for those who don't see us in the same light that we want to see ourselves, but it is still required in each and every sense. Loving others as we love ourselves is the only thing that will change this world. Exclusivism only leads to more exclusivism.

- DAILY DISCIPLINE: DON'T JUST TELL YOUR NEIGHBOR YOU LOVE THEM…DO SOMETHING FOR THEM.

- DAY 77 -
Women's Ministry and Social Activism

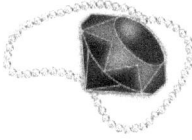

IN THE SAME WAY, TEACH OLDER WOMEN TO BE HOLY [REVERENT] IN THEIR
BEHAVIOR, NOT SPEAKING AGAINST [SLANDERING; GOSSIPING ABOUT]
OTHERS OR ENSLAVED TO TOO MUCH WINE [EXCESSIVE DRINKING],
BUT TEACHING WHAT IS GOOD.
(TITUS 2:3)

- DAILY READING: TITUS 2:1-5

I am the first to admit I tend to avoid women's ministry meetings. To me, they are a gigantic yawn. I am not interested in hearing yet another biased sermon on marriage or what men want in a marriage (especially when no men have been consulted who are under the age of fifty) or what women need to do to keep the men in their lives happy. These images we create of women and what men and women want tend to be colored from another era and not only not applicable, but I also don't know if the ideals they set up for women were ever realistic or what a man "really wants." It is as if I must go and sit through another women's event where we talk about nothing but motherhood, vacuuming, and wearing pink…I am going to lose it.

One thing I have learned by avoiding many women's ministry meetings is that women's ministry can be more than tea parties and big hats on a lazy spring afternoon. Women's ministry and women's ministry meetings can be more than just getting together to look the part of a Christian woman or the concept we have of what being a Christian woman is. If we look at Scripture, the concept of a women's ministry should be to encourage women to be all they can be and to encourage us to do good works, to display our faith, and to live our lives in accord with Gospel principle.

That means we should be women who are willing to get together and do something good for someone else as a part of our women's ministry because it is a part of our faith. We should be women who care about the issues women face worldwide, willing to share from our financial resources as well as our activism, caring about what happens to our communities, our children, our nation, and our sisters who are wherever they may be.

Being a woman should not ever be taught as a one-dimensional experience that revolves around immediate marriage and having children. Many women in the world work hard, do labor that many women in the western world would never imagine doing for themselves. Millions of women worldwide adhere to different social mores and understand the promises and call of women in the Bible very differently than a social call or social meeting where we do product sample giveaways or wear special outfits. We shouldn't think there is only one way to be a woman, or to experience the life of a woman, or only certain things that we can or can't do as women. There are millions of women all over the world who live lives very different from ours who need to know they matter, too, and that their lives are important, just as they are.

So, woman of God, expand your women's ministry to include more than cute get-togethers for women. Do something to help and reach the world, one sister, one woman, at a time. Believe in the promise that being a woman and being one with a group of women behind you is a special thing that can transform the lives of other women, wherever they may be.

- DAILY DISCIPLINE: PICK A SOCIAL PROJECT FOR A WOMEN'S MINISTRY GET-TOGETHER AND BENEFIT THE WORLD AROUND YOU.

- DAY 78 -

Blessed are Those Who are Persecuted...for Doing Right

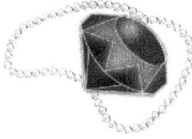

THEY ARE BLESSED WHO ARE PERSECUTED FOR DOING GOOD
[DOING WHAT'S RIGHT; THE SAKE OF RIGHTEOUSNESS], FOR THE KINGDOM
OF HEAVEN BELONGS TO THEM [IS THEIRS].
(MATTHEW 5:10)

- DAILY READING: 1 PETER 4:12-19

All over the world people are persecuted for their beliefs, for trying to maintain right-standing, or for doing the right thing, every day. In the year 2011 alone, intense bouts of violence plagued Nigeria due to the Boko Haram extremist group, the only cabinet-level Christian official in Pakistan was shot, a pastor was sentenced to death for leaving Islam in Iran (even though he was never a Muslim), Coptic Christians in Egypt opened up the new year with a bomb explosion killing at least twenty-two people, church members were arrested in China, Christians building a property in Khartoum, Sudan were attacked, and Christians in Indonesia do not experience adequate protection under the law.[26] Every day, these people live with the realities that today may be their last, even though they are doing nothing but living their lives quietly and peaceably on a daily basis.

Many in the west use the term "persecution" to refer to situations where people do not receive nor accept the message that we bring to them. We are quick to say someone is "persecuting" us because they don't want to hear what we have to say or because they don't agree with us and voice an equally strong position. Yes, we love to have the last word. Oh, we love those moments where we feel like what we have to say has its triumphant moment, and let's take "truth" out of the equation for a moment. We want control of the discussion, we want to be declared "right," and our egos prick when other people don't see things the way we do. That doesn't mean we are being persecuted, not by a long shot. It means we are dealing with and learning how to interact with others, and love other people, as difficult as it may be, and as much as our own personal flesh does not enjoy the process.

We may not understand persecution because we have never experienced it, but that doesn't mean it does not happen. Persecution is a real thing, something unpleasant, and something that changes the way those people view the world and view their faith. It is that place where the rubber meets the road, where someone either believes in what they claim to believe in or they do not, and is either going to stand behind it, or not. That might not sound like a big deal, but in a world where we change our minds like we change our socks and where fear and intimidation are very real things, standing behind one's beliefs and values is an incredible thing in the face of having to lose everything.

People who deal with persecution are those who don't back down, and for this, they are blessed. It comes with a heavenly blessing, something that can't be found in this world or satisfied within it. God Himself looks down on the persecuted and guides their lives and their work, even in the face of hatred, destruction, and death. Surely, we can all learn something from those who are persecuted for their beliefs, because they are the inheritors of all things unseen but spiritually perceived.

- DAILY DISCIPLINE: DO SOME RESEARCH ON PERSECUTED CHRISTIANS IN THE WORLD TODAY.

- Day 79 -
Politics vs. Souls

But treat them just as you treat your own citizens [natives]. Love foreigners [resident aliens] as you love yourselves, because you were foreigners [sojourners; wanderers; resident aliens; Ex. 22:21; Jer. 22:3] one time in Egypt. I am the LORD your God. (Leviticus 19:34)

- Daily Reading: Leviticus 19:32-37

I am a second-generation Italian American, which means I am the second generation of my family to be born in the United States. It might be hard to imagine, but that means prior to my grandparents' generation, nobody ever fathomed life in the United States. In fact, my grandfather was naturalized in 1917, which means my family has barely been in the United States for a century. It doesn't mean we didn't exist prior, but that life for my family was radically different before the long journey to the United States was made, not all that long ago in the scope of history. The long journey to the United States involved living and working in France, Canada, and finally, New York City, where they lived in poverty conditions as laborers for much of their lives.

When my grandparents came over to the United States with their families, there was a push to assimilate into American culture. Their names were changed, their children learned and spoke English rather than the traditional Italian, and subsequent generations went on to marry non-Italians. Nowadays much of Italian culture in America is somewhat of a distant memory, something fast fading from the forefront because the cultural ideals and values were never upheld.

I am the first to admit the questions of immigration are complicated, especially from a political viewpoint. Nations only have so many jobs, so much housing, and so many places for a populace while they maintain both their own unique identity and standard of living. I also can't deny that there is not as much emphasis on assimilation in today's world, thus many people come from other countries while maintaining the ideals and attitudes from their nations of origin. This has the potential to complicate all sorts of things from a cultural and security perspective, and it causes people to raise eyebrows at people who look or dress different from what is perceived to be the "norm." The thing we are not seeing, however, as people and as Christians who operate beyond borders and national identities are that people are people, no matter where they are from and what issues they espouse. While the issues that pertain to immigration may not be simple from a governmental perspective, treating people right and loving your neighbor – no matter where they are from – are always basic principles that we have to espouse when interacting with others.

The church is open to anyone who desires to know more about Jesus Christ and who desire to live in the love of God, no matter where they are from in the world. We are not political people when we step into that church; we are human people. We cannot escape that people created in the image of God and that they have the need for certain things such as food and water, sanitary living conditions, human companionship and stable employment, and that they don't always find those things in their nations of origin. Simple or not, God calls us to look at souls, at needs, and at the essential hearts of people which will never change without Jesus Christ.

- DAILY DISCIPLINE: REACH OUT TO AN IMMIGRANT WHERE YOU LIVE AND FIND OUT IF THERE IS ANYTHING YOU CAN DO FOR THEM.

- DAY 80 -
Woman to Woman

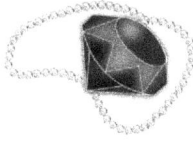

[LISTEN; BEHOLD] THE PAY [WAGES] YOU DID NOT GIVE [DEFRAUDED FROM]
THE WORKERS WHO MOWED YOUR FIELDS CRIES OUT AGAINST YOU
[LEV. 19:13; DEUT. 24:14–15], AND THE CRIES OF THE WORKERS
[HARVESTERS] HAVE BEEN HEARD BY [REACHED THE EARS OF] THE LORD
ALL-POWERFUL [OF HOSTS/ARMIES; SABAOTH; GOD'S WARRIOR NAME
REFERRING TO THE ANGELIC ARMY].
(JAMES 5:4)

- DAILY READING: AMOS 2:6-16

*L*et's talk for a moment, woman to woman. Sure, we like to get together and share our lives and sometimes even share secrets. We like to do lunch, and we like to have our "night out with the girls." We enjoy talking about things that are important to us, and hope that others will find them of value, too. So today, we're going to talk, as women, about something of vital importance: that is called equal opportunity.

The principle behind equal opportunity is that every single person should have the same rights and access to do things, no matter who they are, how old they are, their gender, their national origin, race, religion, or circumstance. It's a great ideal and one that is technically enforced by federal law. The unfortunate reality, however, is that equal opportunity is not something society, nor state law, is built upon. Current statistics state that while Caucasian men make up only 48% of the workforce with a college education, they hold over 90% of the top jobs within the news media, 96% of CEO positions, 86% of partnerships within law firms, and 85% of tenured college faculty jobs.[27] An American woman who works full-time all year is paid only 79 cents for every dollar that is paid to a man.[28] This means women who are maintaining jobs to live, care for families or children, and to sustain life are already at a disadvantage of 21 cents in accomplishing their lives and their goals.

As women, what do we think about this? Do we want this type of life and this type of reality for our daughters who will, one day, grow up and face the same thing? When we tell them that anything is possible, are we just talking, or are we serious – do we genuinely want to make sure that any idea and any desire they have in their hearts is truly possible?

We can lobby and protest about inequalities in the workplace or within general society, and rightly so. Where there are societal inequalities, we should do something about them. But what about the inequalities that exist right within our own households? Do you treat your daughters the same way as you treat your sons? Are girls growing up and dating treated as a catastrophe, whereas boys are given freedoms and liberties the girls are not? Do the girls do "girl chores" and the boys do "boy chores" or are chores done to teach responsibility and home involvement across the board? Are the girls expected to pick up after the boys? Are you always telling the girls about getting married and one day having children while you tell the boys about being all they can be, seeing the world and going to school?

As women, equal opportunity starts with every single one of us and the way we teach our daughters to want as much as our boys. It starts when we encourage their dreams and give them messages about changing the world around them and being all they can be, just as they are. Are we loving our daughters, or are we just waiting until the time when they get married? The choice is ours.

- DAILY DISCIPLINE: IF YOU ARE DUE FOR A RAISE, PETITION FOR ONE. IF YOU ARE AN EMPLOYER, PAY YOUR EMPLOYEES EQUALLY.

- DAY 81 -
Being Real About Marriage

BUT [HOWEVER; IN ANY CASE; OR TO SUM UP] EACH ONE OF YOU MUST LOVE HIS WIFE AS HE LOVES HIMSELF, AND A WIFE MUST RESPECT [REVERENCE; V. 21] HER HUSBAND.
(EPHESIANS 5:33)

- DAILY READING: EPHESIANS 5:21-33

Marriage and dating are two topics I like to avoid when people come to me for prayer. I believe there is a fine line between decreeing and declaring and witchcraft, and I meet too many people who want me to pray that a mate will magically manifest in their lives. They don't seek God's will or desire to seek God about marriage or about living with a mate or about resolving the things within themselves that are going to help them to be a better mate with a better relationship outlook. Come to me and ask for prayer for that, rather than praying into existence a man or woman who is "perfect" for you and, therefore, does not really exist.

Yes, I know where I am going today is going to make many of us uncomfortable. Within my own scope of opinion, marriage is not a social cause, but so many have turned it into that, I can't help but devote some time to some introspection on marriage. We know divorce rates are up; we also know marital unhappiness is up. Considering people stayed together because they felt they had to and we don't really know how people felt about their marriages in days gone by, I don't know the state of marriage is really all that different from how it has ever been. That doesn't mean we can't do something to make it better, and doing something to make it better doesn't start with my prayers to find you the perfect mate or to change who you live with. The best way we can improve marital odds is to be real about ourselves and to make sure we give a consistent message in who we are to our mate.

See, when we think we want to get married, we start giving off all sort of unstable, inconsistent vibrations about who we really are. Giving a consistent message about who we are not only shows that we know who we are and what we are looking for, it gives our mate the opportunity to decide if we are what they are looking for. This might sound simplistic, and in some ways, it certainly is. If you start playing relationship games, such as hard-to-get, or trying to conform to what you feel is the proper Christian form for a man or woman when that is not who you really are or how you really feel, all you are going to do is mislead someone and create a destructive, toxic circumstance in your relationship. When the "real you" comes out, the other person is not going to know how to handle things because they aren't going to have any idea who "you" really is. This means many relationships end, situations end, and marriages fail because people don't know who they are and, thus, they don't know how to interact when things come into focus through reality.

Games, expectations, miscommunicating on purpose, and relationship rules do nothing but make sure that everyone plays along just long enough to create something completely and totally dishonest. My best relationship advice? Be yourself. Who you are needs to come out sooner rather than later so everyone can love and be loved for themselves, not what someone else hopes they might be.

- DAILY DISCIPLINE: COME CLEAN ABOUT WHO YOU ARE IN YOUR RELATIONSHIPS, SHOWING YOUR PARTNER THE "REAL YOU."

- DAY 82 -
We're all the Same Kind of Different

I WILL BRING THESE PEOPLE TO MY HOLY MOUNTAIN AND GIVE THEM JOY IN MY HOUSE OF PRAYER. THE OFFERINGS AND SACRIFICES THEY PLACE ON MY ALTAR WILL PLEASE ME [BE ACCEPTED], BECAUSE MY TEMPLE WILL BE CALLED A HOUSE FOR PRAYER FOR PEOPLE FROM ALL NATIONS [MATT. 21:13; MARK 11:17; LUKE 19:46]."
(ISAIAH 56:7)

- DAILY READING: 1 CORINTHIANS 12:12-26

I already mentioned in an earlier devotion that as I write this, it is an election year. In fact, as I write this specific devotion, we are only about six weeks away from the presidential election. We have two candidates on the platform following what has been a complicated and disgraceful campaigning experience, to say the least. One politician has extensive experience in politics, including experience working on the White House cabinet, while another has come in, out of the blue, with no political experience, but extensive years in business and entertainment. To many, the choice seems obvious who the better candidate is for president. To others, however, the choice doesn't seem quite so clear.

I've long wondered why this election doesn't seem to be a simple, cut-and-dry situation to voters. After talking about something with someone else today, I figured it out. One candidate understands the complicated nature of politics and of our society today. Things are not simple; in fact, they are complicated beyond reasonable measure. As the intricate nature of the human being rears its head more and more, we are learning that people don't fit into categories or classifications as easily as we might like them to. In acknowledging this, it brings into focus and reality the fact that life is not what it once was, and probably never was that to begin with. With this other candidate, the way in which they move operates by compartmentalizing people and things into categories. The method the candidate uses sounds simple enough:

165

let's do this for this group, this for this group, handle this group this way, and handle this group that way. There's no consideration for individuals or rights, only sweeping generalizations that seem to make life something easy, obtainable and controllable.

It might sound appealing to neatly compartmentalize and generalize about people, saying this will be law or that will be illegal, but the realities about life (and politics) and human beings are that we can't stick people into generalized categories and consider it good thinking or a simpler way of life. Every one of us is, as I call it, "the same kind of different." We have general needs that need to be acknowledged and general rights that need to be upheld, but beyond these basic statements, the generalizations end. Our perspectives on life and living vary, and trying too hard to fit everyone into one category or one statement makes it much more difficult to reach and interact with others.

Some people think the Bible contradicts itself; I believe the Bible shows us the reality that not every situation fits into the same category and that different circumstances often call for different answers. If we can open ourselves up to recognize these facts, it makes it far easier to embrace the differences that others have and embrace our own, as well. God does not expect us to be carbon copies, and neither should we. Hard or challenging, this is the world we are in…and we will only transform it by love.

- DAILY DISCIPLINE: EXPLORE THE WAY THAT YOUR SPIRITUAL GIFTS WORK IN COMBINATION WITH THOSE OF OTHERS.

- DAY 83 -
The Blame Game

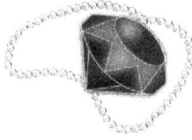

JESUS ANSWERED, "IT IS NOT THIS MAN'S SIN OR HIS PARENTS' SIN THAT MADE
HIM BLIND. THIS MAN WAS BORN BLIND SO THAT GOD'S POWER [WORKS]
COULD BE SHOWN [DISPLAYED; REVEALED; MANIFEST] IN HIM."
(JOHN 9:3)

- DAILY READING: JOHN 9:1-12

When the AIDS crisis broke out, it seemed like everyone had an opinion about who had it and why they had it. The automatic assumption was (and most of the time, still is) that someone who has HIV was gay and contracted the disease for that reason. It's amazing how oblivious people are to the facts about HIV, the number of different ways someone can contract the virus, and that viruses don't discriminate or segregate themselves to specific demographics of people. There is a pervasive and long-lasting message that people who have HIV deserve to have it, and they have it because they did something to deserve it.

Now we fast-forward for so many years and it's no longer just HIV that's the blame-game culprit. Any time someone is sick, especially with a terminal disease such as cancer, the person who has the disease is blamed for having it. They are accused of doing something wrong at some point in their lives, of God not loving them or somehow doing something to "deserve" being ill. If someone isn't healed immediately, they are accused of not having enough faith or of being sick because they don't have faith in healing. Over and over again, I hear the same victim shaming that we do with so many different circumstances in life. Someone is sick, so they have done something to deserve it, and instead of praying and seeking God on their behalf, we are going to use faith to criticize and condemn them for it.

People get sick because we live in a fallen world where we are susceptible to illness and physical malady. HIV, AIDS, cancer, diabetes, miscarriages, Multiple Sclerosis, and other ailments do not exist in

167

people's lives because they are doing something wrong. They aren't a blight or a punishment for sins. They are not a sign of secret, hidden sin. Illnesses happen because they do, and because they often don't have a specific answer or deep-rooted cause, that makes them harder and more difficult to endure. That means as people go through their season of question, doubt, physical discomfort and physical illness, we need to be there for them, even more.

We need to stop thinking that an illness tells us everything about another person or gives us some sort of secret insight into people's personal lives. Illness is hard enough without having to feel like everyone around you is judging you and speaking badly about you, both behind your back and to your face. In illness, it is important to feel the comfort, the reassurance and the promise of feeling God's presence in such a difficult time.

For the sick around you, be an individual who feels God's love, health, and healing in each and every hug you give to them. Be a comforting resource, a person who makes that difference and who lets someone know: they aren't sick because they did something...they aren't sick because they missed God...they are in a situation that merits our love and compassion.

- DAILY DISCIPLINE: PRAY FOR SOMEONE'S HEALING WITHOUT JUDGMENT OR CRITICISM.

- DAY 84 -
The Oil of Joy for Mourning

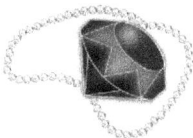

I WILL GIVE THEM...THE OIL OF GLADNESS [JOY] TO REPLACE THEIR SORROW [MOURNING]...
(ISAIAH 61:3)

- DAILY READING: PSALM 126:1-6

*I*f you walked into a funeral and started pouring oil over everyone's heads, most mourners would think you were insensitive at best, and in need of mental health counseling, at worst. Running into a moment reserved for grief, proclaiming that you were giving all of the mourners "the oil of joy" while pouring it upon them wouldn't seem like something that screamed proper etiquette. Even though God might not advise we handle ourselves in this exact manner, part of His proclamation to His people is just that – the oil of joy in place of mourning.

Many modern and conventional viewpoints condemn the mourning process. We are told it's good to be happy, happiness is equivalent to joy, and we should never go through things in life that cause us to experience sadness. The problem with this kind of thinking is that mourning is a part of life. As long as we live on this side of heaven, we will experience loss, which will lead us to mourn. That means whenever we look at the experience of mourning, we should see what the result will be. The Bible promises that as we trade our mourning for something more, we will receive the oil of joy.

Oil almost always represents the anointing in the Bible, or the purposed, God-established commission upon the life of those He calls and choses for His work. Have you ever stopped to think about why oil is used to signify this, instead of something else? For example, why isn't water, which has great spiritual significance, used? Why isn't wine, which also is used throughout the Scriptures, used? Why is it consistently shown to us as oil? I believe oil has certain attributes that clarify why oil is something used to display the anointing: it must be crushed and pressed, it has a golden color which points to eternal and heavenly things, and it moves and flows slowly, rather than quickly, when it is poured. Oil has a flow to it, commanding its presence and a movement that is longer lasting and more permanent than other liquids that could be used.

This means the oil of joy pours over our lives and moves in such a way that is not only noticeable, it displays the grandeur of God's call and purpose within us. Joy comes forth from applied pressure, from all those things that come along to crush us and destroy us, but God has different plans in such opposition. The things that seemingly break us, causing us to mourn and to grieve our losses, cause a pressure to erupt in our lives that breaks forth the oil that leads us to joy. Joy is not happiness, as happiness is fleeting and changeable, but joy is a constant, purposed assurance that causes us to overflow in gratitude and praise for all God is and all we are to become.

In mourning, we come to know God: the aspects of living in God and dealing with spiritual things that are less than pleasant and difficult. In those times, He comforts and cares for us, leading us to the place of unending joy.

- DAILY DISCIPLINE: BE AN AGENT OF JOY TO SOMEONE ELSE.

- Day 85 -
Act Justly, Love Mercy, and Walk Humbly With God

The LORD has told you, human [O man], what is good;
He has told you what He wants [the LORD requires] from you:
to do what is right to other people [just], love being kind
to others [mercy; lovingkindness], and live humbly, obeying
[walk humbly with] your God.
(Micah 6:8)

- DAILY READING: MICAH 6:1-8

I first saw Micah 6:8 on my Catholic junior high school's weekly newsletter. I would probably venture it is safe to say I'd probably never heard of the book of Micah, let alone know any of it with any assurance to recite verses from it or recognize the verse when I saw it. There was something about it, however, that called me to attention. The principle that what God requires of His people is quite simple and summarized in a three-fold manner: to act justly, love mercy, and walk humbly with Him, made sense to me. It was a verse that stuck with me all throughout my life now, and down to the present day, especially when tackling some complicated and intense topics in the Bible. Studying the Old Testament, especially the complications of the law and the prophets, can make God sound complicated and that what He requires of us is complicated. How could anyone ever make sense out of the law, let alone try to follow the whole thing? How could the Israelites make sure they were following every part of it right? What happened if someone didn't follow it right because they didn't understand it?

The book of Micah's contents echoes those of other Minor Prophets, just in a little different way. Living in a bloody and violent time within the history of Israel, Micah turned his attention to the many ways the people who claimed to be of God were failing God in ways they never considered. Those ways related to social justices and injustices that had become such a major part of the people's lives, they didn't consider them infractions anymore. If they did consider them, they made sure to excuse away the ways they stole, lied, swindled, and extorted money from others as well as mistreating and abusing those around them.

Thus, the purpose of Micah's words wasn't to re-state the law; they were to clarify to God's people that they could follow all those little parts of the law they felt they understood well enough to distort and manipulate and still be displeasing in His sight. Social justice matters before God and how we treat one another matters to Him more than how perfect we try to be and appear in this life. The summary of what God wanted was simple: no, you might not figure it all out, but the bottom line was to act justly (reflect God's character of assessment in your life), love mercy (have a heart of forgiveness and kindness when dealing with others) and walk humbly (esteeming one's self properly, not more than someone else, and not less) with God.

It wasn't complicated then, and it's not complicated now. God is not asking us to try and re-instate Old Testament law, because doing so shows we don't rightly understand the work of Christ nor of love and grace in our lives. Rather, He expects that by walking in His Spirit and having a sense of purpose, we are to exemplify a sense of social justice, divine social justice rather than worldly justice, within our lives. If we act justly, love mercy, and walk humbly, we can change the world.

- DAILY DISCIPLINE: FIND AN ACTIVITY THAT PROMOTES JUSTICE, MERCY, AND HUMILITY, AND BECOME A PART OF THE WORK THAT IS BEING DONE.

- DAY 86 -
Limitless Ministry

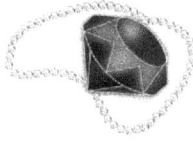

THE LORD SAID TO ABRAM, "LEAVE YOUR COUNTRY, YOUR RELATIVES,
AND YOUR FATHER'S FAMILY [HOUSE], AND GO TO THE LAND
I WILL SHOW YOU [CANAAN, THE PROMISED LAND]."
(GENESIS 12:1)

- DAILY READING: JOHN 3:16-21

*I*n my nearly twenty years of ministry, I have met ministers who have never seen the outside of a church. Some of them have been in ministry for as long or longer than me. Their entire concept of what God can and will do is within the boundaries of a church, on a Sunday morning, during a church service. If God is going to move, He's going to have to move according to schedule and not run over time by any stretch of the imagination. If anyone wants to get the touch of God they seek, they are going to have to do it during the weekly service. The church is closed and locked the rest of the week, with no one on staff available, and no one available by phone. If you want God, and if God wants you, that meeting will have to happen during the regularly scheduled service. There is no outreach, no engagement with others, and if an outsider fails to follow the prescribed rules, that person will not be welcome.

This is an extreme example (and based in fact, by the way) of the ways we limit God when we are in ministry. There is a great temptation to get comfortable in ministry and start thinking God operates exclusively by the means we operate or flow in most easily. I certainly don't want to give the impression that preaching is an easy thing to do, not by a longshot. But it is easy to adapt the mentality that where we are most at ease and most comfortable – in a church, full of believers, who applaud us and give us money – is the only place God has for us to be.

Ministry is service and what we do in ministry should always stretch us and stretch our limits beyond what is comfortable and what we feel we know best. With God, we are touching eternity and touching lives by bringing them into a place of total eternity. The whole idea that we are touching and tapping into eternity as we make eternity real in light of existing temporal problems means we are offering something beyond our comfortable limits. The work of ministry should always challenge us to do more, go farther, and touch more lives. Never, ever should we think God starts and ends in a church building or service or that we should expect people to meet us in church to find God. It's fine to invite people to church, but we can't expect encounters with God only happen when we are there. If we understand God to be omnipresent, God can show up and show out wherever He so desires. If we are His stewards, then it should be our desire to serve God wherever He desires to show His presence.

Don't be afraid of doing different things in ministry. Don't fear the limitless nature of ministry that can take you beyond anything you'd ever imagine God as able to do through you. Soar beyond convention, beyond the boundaries of denominational rules, and beyond the concepts and ideas that you've had about God that keep you bound and boxed in. Sometimes we are as bound as those we try to help…we just don't realize it until we remove the limits.

- DAILY DISCIPLINE: FELLOWSHIP WITH A MINISTRY THAT HAS AN INTERNATIONAL PRESENCE.

- DAY 87 -
Choosing Choice

BUT GOD KNOWS THE WAY THAT I TAKE, AND WHEN HE HAS TESTED ME,
I WILL COME OUT LIKE GOLD [PS. 139:23-24].
(JOB 23:10)

- DAILY READING: MATTHEW 7:1-6

Whenever the term "choice" is used in politics it usually relates to issues of abortion, birth control, and healthcare for women. This means when people talk about "choice" they automatically think of it in those limited terms, thinking only of the ways it relates to those specific issues. The truth is when it comes to choice in politics and choice in life, we tend to eschew the issues and misunderstand what they mean. Being pro-choice doesn't mean someone thinks everyone should run out and have an abortion, or that people should never desire to have children. It means the decisions about these things belong to the woman and not her government or elected officials. These aren't the only areas where choice is misunderstood or makes us uncomfortable as people, however. I believe the concept of choice makes us uncomfortable as a rule because if we understand people have the right to make their own choices, that means we don't have control over what they want to do.

Human nature, the flesh, the part of us that is not redeemed and fights our redemption, loves the idea of being in control. We want everyone to do what we want and follow the principles we think are best. We can be the biggest mess imaginable, unable to make our own choices, and unable to make good decisions, but we think we know best for everyone else. We want to give advice, we want to go beyond advice-giving into the area of being outright bossy and demanding, and when people respond in a negative way, we get angry at them. We might stop speaking to them for find every reason in the book to judge them for their decision, because we don't respect that they have that right – that need – to make a decision for themselves.

Life is full of people making choices that we don't agree about or ascribe to support. It's unrealistic to believe we are going to bully people into our viewpoints by mandating their choices align with our beliefs. Even if you have been in a similar situation at some point in time, you aren't that person, walking out their experience and feeling what they feel about their situation. You don't know the personal odds and personal experiences they encounter while assessing their options. You also don't know how they will respond with any of the outcomes they face. Only they know that and can imagine that because they are the ones dealing with their decisions.

Choosing choice gives you the unique opportunity to be there for others because you support their identity as an individual. Even though they might make a mistake, you will still be there because you love them and recognize they need to make their own decisions, on their own. Supporting the principle of choice means you know we get better with decision-making through experience, and we need to be people who stand behind others whether their choices are good or bad, easy or difficult, and whether they go awry, or stay the same. Choose choice. It gives you the opportunity to love others...regardless.

- DAILY DISCIPLINE: RESPECT OTHER'S CHOICES BY SUPPORTING THEM REGARDLESS OF THE DECISIONS THEY MAKE.

- DAY 88 -

God Changes not...But We Need to

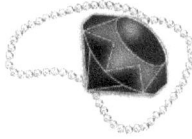

I THE LORD DO NOT CHANGE. SO YOU DESCENDANTS OF JACOB
HAVE NOT BEEN DESTROYED [CONSUMED].
(MALACHI 3:6)

- DAILY READING: MATTHEW 3:1-10

The concept of a perfect God is intimidating to many of us. That is because we put our own spin on what it means to be perfect, our human concept of perfection that leaves us with a profound sense of lack. To us, being perfect means never making any mistakes, always looking the part, sounding the part, acting the part, and properly doing what needs to be done, whenever it needs to be done. Perfection sounds like the ultimate achievement, and it is something we go to great lengths to appear as if we have found, even though we haven't. We like to look like we've got it all together, the ultimate image of perfection, but no matter how hard we try, we don't.

That's because perfection, as we understand it in a spiritual sense, is not what is real in our fallen concept of perfection. Living in a fallen world, we don't readily accept the fact that our perfection is unobtainable this side of heaven and that we go through different cycles and customs that merit change. We, as people, no matter how good we look on the surface or how hard we try to look the right part, are not now, nor will ever be perfect and we are going to be called to change throughout our lives.

There is no such thing as perfect doctrine and we will never have a perfect understanding of spiritual, political, social, or life truth. That's because we are seeing it all from down here, from the tainted viewpoint that doesn't recognize true perfection. God doesn't change because God is perfect, and that means the true understanding of perfection is the reality of a Being that is all-understanding, all-knowing, all-embracing, and yes, all-consuming. God doesn't need to change because He already knows the end from the beginning and has already crossed into the differences that come about because of our change.

What seems like change to us is us aligning ourselves to God's never-changing reality. It is change for us but fitting into God's greater plan within spiritual perception. God is. He is outside of time and space, and He is as much in yesterday as He is right now and already in tomorrow. We are called within change to align to eternity, to true reality, in a greater sense, in a bigger way than we can imagine.

In the context of social activism and reform, we need to look at the areas we hold dear that are most in need of change. Sometimes the very things that hold us back from being true advocates and making true change are the traditions, ideals, and concepts we hold most dear to our heart. The activity of the Holy Spirit ensures we are relevant for today, and yet our own unwillingness to flow, to move as the breath of wind that shows up in one place that we cannot see, is what keeps us from doing the work that most needs to be done in this time and place. God changes not, but we need to. We need to more than words can express because if we refuse to change and touch eternity, we are willfully refusing to be relevant in the here and now.

- DAILY DISCIPLINE: DON'T ASSUME YOU DON'T NEED TO CHANGE. JUST CHANGE.

- DAY 89 -
A Garment of Praise for the Spirit of Heaviness

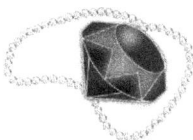

I WILL GIVE...CLOTHES [A GARMENT] OF PRAISE TO REPLACE THEIR SPIRIT
OF SADNESS [DISCOURAGEMENT; HEAVY HEART].
(ISAIAH 61:3)

- DAILY READING: 1 PETER 5:6-11

I love clothes, I love shoes, and I love fashion. I didn't start out this way. I went to Catholic school during some formative years, so I was rather turned off by the entire concept of fashion. We wore a standard navy blue, light blue, and white uniform that screamed loudly of Catholic school plaid. We were told what we had to wear down to our shoes and socks, and we were prohibited from wearing jewelry, make-up, and nail polish. They even had regulations on acceptable hair styles! It wasn't until years later that I realized much of the conformity we experienced in our attire related to vocational preparation (the hopes we would desire to become priests or nuns). Self-expression was a big, huge no-no in all its forms.

As an adult, I have grown to love fashion because it is that self-expression I lacked in Catholic school. The type of clothes we wear can say so much about us as people. I know clothing is often used as a status symbol, but that's not the context I am talking about. The style of clothes we like, the colors we choose, the fit of our garments, what we find comfortable, the patterns that interest us, and the nature of our clothes reveal interests, hopes, desires, likes, and dislikes. In our clothing tells a story of who we are and where we want to be.

If there is self-expression in our natural garments, there is great expression in our spiritual garments, as well. When the Scriptures speak of us putting on a garment of one thing or another, it means we take on an attribute and clothe ourselves in it, wrapping ourselves from head to toe in that expression. In this example, we can clothe ourselves in the garment of praise as we trade in the spirit of heaviness, which is also something that can be worn. If we are wearing the spirit of heaviness, it reflects in a heavy countenance. We might be sad or depressed, and we are walking around, holding something upon us that weighs us down and damages our image of right, wrong, others, and ourselves. When we clothe ourselves with that, from head-to-toe, or deal with someone who is clothed like that, the only answer is to take it off! But what do we put on in its place?

We are told that God gives us a garment of praise for the spirit of heaviness. We can wear one or the other; only one can be our form of self-expression. We can't wear heaviness and praise at the same time. To put on a garment of praise means to wear praise as if it is our garment, clothing ourselves in it and letting praise stand as our statement. Praise represents a place of freedom, one where we are not bound by the things that lead us to live our lives full of heaviness.

We live in a world that needs to discover praise, to cast off the spirit of heaviness and experience freedom from all the wrongs of this world that have them bound. To bring that message of change, wrap yourself in the spirit of praise for truth.

- DAILY DISCIPLINE: START A "PRAISE JOURNAL" AND THINK OF AT LEAST ONE THING EVERYDAY THAT INSPIRES YOU TO PRAISE GOD.

- DAY 90 -
Revolutionary Spirits

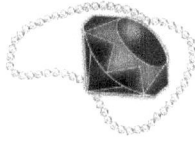

JOHN [THE BAPTIST] WAS BAPTIZING PEOPLE IN THE DESERT [WILDERNESS] AND PREACHING A BAPTISM OF CHANGED HEARTS AND LIVES [TURNING FROM SIN; REPENTANCE] FOR THE FORGIVENESS [REMISSION] OF SINS.
(MARK 1:4)

- DAILY READING: MARK 1:9-13

Do you love conformity? If you do, you aren't alone. Most people like the idea of doing the same things as everyone else because change is scary to them. There is something comfortable about going with the flow, even if we know the flow is moving in a bad direction. We might know the trend is wrong and the general concept and ideas of the direction aren't moving in the right direction, but we don't want to stand out from the crowd. Doing so might mean people change their opinions of us and it might mean our social status changes. We like fitting in and knowing what is coming next.

Realizing this within ourselves should give us greater respect for those revolutionary spirits who changed the world as both they knew it and as we knew it. It takes a special person willing to break with conformity and the comforts of a safe reputation to stand out from among the crowd and be counted.

One of these revolutionary spirits who changed the world forever was John the Baptist. Before we started naming churches and religious orders after John, he was a wild-looking man with a strange diet who came out of unknown territory with an equally unknown message. As he went about the countryside calling the religious and non-religious alike to repentance, he didn't go carrying a Bible while in an expensive blue suit and tie with a caravan of fifteen armor bearers behind him. He braved the new and unknown world alone, just him and God, with a message he knew God gave to him.

We don't have to be people who run off by ourselves with every idea that crosses our minds. John most likely came from a community that embraced intense discipline and Scriptural study. He didn't preach revolution from his own ideas or thoughts that randomly occurred to him. He spent years in discipline and insight, learning to hear the voice of God because he was a prophet. He knew that the time was ready for the revolution and that he was here for this time, this place, right now.

That is the essence of a revolutionary spirit: they are a person who knows the time is now and the place is here. We don't have another moment, day, or year to stay the same, because the longer we stay the same, the longer we won't see the growth and change needed to move society toward a better day.

Every one of us should not just pray to meet and find revolutionary spirits in our time...we should pray for the courage of conviction and the integrity of heart to be revolutionary spirits. Whenever we see wrong, we need to speak up about it. We should be willing to stand with those who stand up against the wrong of society and usher in a new day. Instead of having a fear of being different, we should fear being and staying the same. Ahead of their time, revolutionary spirits tap into a world that we are not in just yet, but desperately need to be.

- DAILY DISCIPLINE: SPEAK UP AGAINST THE WRONG AROUND YOU INSTEAD OF GOING WITH THE CROWD.

- DAY 91 -
Where is the God of Justice?

LORD, HOW LONG MUST I ASK [CRY; CALL] FOR HELP AND YOU IGNORE [DO NOT HEAR] ME? I CRY OUT TO YOU ABOUT VIOLENCE [OR "VIOLENCE!"], BUT YOU DO NOT SAVE [RESCUE] US!
(HABAKKUK 1:2)

- DAILY READING: AMOS 5:18-27

*J*ustice is the theory by which a right situation is set in motion and properly declared. I think it's important that when we talk about justice, even within its understanding, it is a "theory." It is something that is supposed to exist in circumstances that warrant it, but being a theory, it doesn't always manifest like we might want it to. If you watch the modern-day news or study history, you know the execution of justice is, most likely, lacking much of the time. Those who need it the most don't see it or experience it and those who are the perpetrators of injustice are often those who claim it for themselves.

In 1850, Ebenezer Elliott was disturbed by the abuses and injustices he saw in his nation at the time. He cried out to God and penned a poem that we now know as the hymn, "God Save The People." It has been best immortalized as one of the early songs in the musical *Godspell*, but before it was a song that pictures people hearing the preaching of Jesus and coming to follow Him, it was a protest hymn. The poem fought to repeal the British Corn Laws that caused hardship and starvation among the poor, and led him to be known as the "Corn Law rhymer."[28] The second verse of the poem (now hymn) reads:

> Shall crime bring crime for ever,
> Strength aiding still the strong?
> Is it Thy will, O Father,
> That man shall toil for wrong?

"No," say Thy mountains; "No," Thy skies;
Man's clouded sun shall brightly rise,
And songs be heard instead of sighs;
God save the people![30]

When you are faced with the injustices of an era, it's a natural, human question to ask where God is. We don't understand how God works all the time, and looking around and seeing the realities of injustice can cause us to feel frustrated. The catch is, God doesn't cause injustice, nor does He perpetrate it. As humans, sin entered the picture because we insisted on going our own way, demanding our own spiritual and intellectual separation. We wanted to be independent and now we got it. That means the results of injustice come not from God, but from us not drawing close enough to God to embrace the realities that wrongs need to be made right and that we need to stand with a concept of fairness and equity that we can't find through our own means. Yes, until we are willing to step back and admit that we fail, we will always miss the God of justice, Who dries every tear and stands with those who have been mistreated.

- DAILY DISCIPLINE: WRITE A POEM IN PROTEST OF INJUSTICES THAT YOU SEE TODAY.

- DAY 92 -

Return Love for Great Hatred

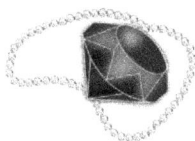

IF SOMEONE DOES WRONG TO YOU, DO NOT PAY HIM BACK BY DOING
WRONG TO HIM [REPAY NO ONE EVIL FOR EVIL]. TRY TO DO
[OR CONSIDER CAREFULLY] WHAT EVERYONE THINKS IS RIGHT
[OTHERS VIEW AS GOOD/HONORABLE; IS GOOD/NOBLE BEFORE ALL PEOPLE].
(ROMANS 12:17)

- DAILY READING: 1 JOHN 4:13-21

*T*he first official year of Sanctuary International Fellowship Tabernacle – SIFT was challenging, to say the least. I won't lie and say I knew what I was doing in totality, because I wasn't. God desired me to have a certain experience in that year to give me better insight into what I was asking others to do in their training with the church. There were things I'd never thought of before that I needed to be aware of. I went from a minister who had always had church in her home and at conferences or preached in other people's churches to a full-time, in-house preacher with a church to maintain and bills to pay. I started with two families, one of which was my own, and one of which was headed by a woman who expressed interest in training to be a pastor. She came from a ministry with a questionable reputation and a leader who was then in prison, serving a year-long sentence for larceny, and was far more involved with that leader than she let on. One of the things she brought with her were very questionable ordination credentials from that former ministry, and insisted she was called to ministry. She was not, at the time, accused nor charged with any wrongdoing, and I've always believed in redemption. She admitted the former leader was a bad fit and wanted a new start, a new change.

Over time, it was obvious she wasn't as motivated to achieve the new start she desired. She began withdrawing from services and found herself uninterested in completing projects. She also began displaying a "know-it-all" attitude and arguing during services or Bible studies. I also knew she was talking behind my back and saying things that were less than stellar when I was not around. I had dealt with this type of thing before, and my typical style of handling such things usually involved stern confrontation while pulling the metaphorical rug out from under the individual. This time, God didn't let me do that. The more difficult she got, the more I was to show her fairness and love, and act like she wasn't doing what she was doing. The more she acted ugly and hateful, the more I had to love her.

This was maybe harder than it sounds, and it sounds pretty hard, so imagine being in a situation where you had to do it! I had moments where I would look out at the congregation and want to say something or call her on things she was doing, but I would stop myself and realize that returning hatred for her hatred is exactly what she wanted. She wanted me to yell and scream, making a big fuss and throwing a huge fit so she could act even uglier with justification.

Yes, this woman left the ministry, in a huge huff, about ten months after we started. It wasn't because she got her way, however, it was because I didn't give it to her. Some things need to be starved and hatred is one of them. Returning hate for hate just breeds hate. Returning love for hate may not mean you get love in return, but it definitely means your hatred isn't what continues to fuel their own.

- DAILY DISCIPLINE: INSTEAD OF RETALIATING AGAINST SOMEONE WHO HAS SHOWED YOU HATE, SHOW THEM LOVE.

- DAY 93 -
Teaching our Children

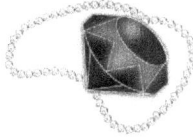

TRAIN CHILDREN TO LIVE THE RIGHT WAY [IN THEIR/OR HIS PATH; REFERRING EITHER TO CHILDREN OR TO GOD], AND WHEN THEY ARE OLD, THEY WILL NOT STRAY [DEPART] FROM IT.
(PROVERBS 22:6)

- DAILY READING: ISAIAH 54:11-15

*I*t seems like it might as well have been 50 years ago, but it hasn't been that many since I was a kid. When I was a kid, going to school was a big deal. Getting educated was a big deal. Having life experiences to teach us essential things about life was a big deal. Being a kid meant learning and getting educated. I grew up before we had cell phones, home computers were a rarity before I hit junior high, and we'd never dreamed of this thing we now call the internet. Social media was nonexistent, and we spent our free time fighting over phone calls once we got old enough to make them and playing by ourselves, with siblings, or with friends. This all came after homework, of course, and chores.

It disturbs me now to see people who have come after me (as well as children today) who did not grow up with that central importance of learning in their lives. Discussions online show children do not have a basis of where they have come from or their life history. 13% of high school seniors show any solid academic understanding of American history. As students get younger, the numbers are comparable: 22% of fourth graders and 18% of eighth graders show any proficiency in the subject.[31]

Learning is about more than just the mere prospect of making sure we don't repeat history over and over again. Making sure our children have a solid foundation and understanding of who they are and where they come from helps them to understand themselves and to explore more of what interests them. In order to have wings, we must first have roots. We must see people went through things to give us the life we now claim as our own and embrace that as an appreciative pull. Our children need to know more than a Sunday school lesson or a few Bible verses to make it in life; they need to know who they are.

I've often said I wonder where the reformers of our era are, those who do the things they do to make a difference and to stand for something. In the past generations, artists, reformers, musicians, and others made known their unconventional and often controversial viewpoints through their art forms. Their goal was to express themselves through their art, not just to make money. Now I see children who think they want to be reality television stars or hip-hop artists because they believe they are "rich and famous," but fail to see there is often substance lacking in their own art forms because they haven't learned enough in life to know there is more to life than money.

If we don't teach our children, nobody else will. If we don't show them where they come from, they won't know who they are. It is our job to help our children discover their inner voice. To do that, they need to hear the stories of generations past echo in their heads so they will discover how they can make a difference in this generation, right now.

- DAILY DISCIPLINE: TAKE AN INTEREST IN WHAT IS TAUGHT IN YOUR LOCAL SCHOOL SYSTEM.

- DAY 94 -
Being a Woman of Valor

GIVE HER THE REWARD SHE HAS EARNED [FRUIT OF HER HANDS];
SHE SHOULD BE PRAISED IN PUBLIC [THE GATES; 31:23] FOR WHAT
SHE HAS DONE.
(PROVERBS 31:31)

- DAILY READING: PROVERBS 31:10-31

The Proverbs 31 woman. Don't we all love her…or is it that we love/hate her? Every time it's time for a women's meeting, a Mother's Day sermon, a women's conference, or something themed around women, the Proverbs 31 woman shows up. She doesn't have a name or a face, but somehow, every woman in that room is measuring themselves up against a woman they never met. Of course, they never measure up. She sounds so perfect, so holy, so competent, the Proverbs 31 woman is the surest way to make you feel like a worthless piece of nothing. You can walk in feeling great, and the second you leave, you're ready to throw in the towel and become a hermit.

The truth about the Proverbs 31 woman is that she was never intended to make women feel badly about themselves. In Orthodox Judaism, Proverbs 31 is considered a song of praise that men sing to their wives in honor of all the things wives and mothers do for their husbands and families.[32] It was never understood to be a long "to-do" list and it was certainly never meant to be the central and exclusive theme for all things female in church. It also has a decidedly militant nature in the Hebrew that does not translate in the English. The proper term for the "virtuous woman," as we call her, is actually "woman of valor," which means she is a woman who lives personally brave, strong in mind and spirit, and is fit to encounter danger.

God does not just call us to be women of valor; He has duly equipped us to be women of valor. The ability to stand in the battle, brave and strong, steadfast and firm, is within us because we are His.

189

We can stand strong, not approaching life as a huge to-do or to-don't list, but as an adventure that demands our sincerity and purpose.

Women of valor stand for something; they stand for what is right. They don't back down in the impression of fear or reputation. A woman who is duly positioned and purposed for her assignment should not fear people retaliating or judging her as not being "ladylike" or improper. If you are there, and here for this time, you do not have to be a prissy, quiet, demure woman who never says anything and always falls behind. Being a true woman of valor means stepping up and doing the job that needs to be done, no matter how difficult of a task it may be. There is no "I don't know" or "I am going to wait for a man to do the job" when you are a woman of valor. It's now or never, and a true woman knows that it's now, because it'll never be never.

A part of us likes the image of women as pristine and untouched, never fettered or aggressive. The problem with this image is that the world created it, owns it, and has put its own stamp on it. If we want to be God's women, triumphant of valor, we have to be willing to get a little down and dirty to be real and reach the world with a message they can't find in a prissy, pristine woman.

- DAILY DISCIPLINE: BE THE WOMAN GOD HAS CREATED YOU TO BE INSTEAD OF AN ABSTRACT CONCEPT OF WOMANHOOD PUSHED BY CHRISTIAN CHURCHES.

- DAY 95 -
Violated by Trust

THE ENEMY [THEY] ABUSED [VIOLATED; RAPED] THE WOMEN OF JERUSALEM
[IN ZION; THE LOCATION OF THE TEMPLE] AND THE GIRLS [VIRGINS]
IN THE CITIES [TOWNS] OF JUDAH.
(LAMENTATIONS 5:11)

- DAILY READING: GENESIS 34:1-7

ape is never a comfortable topic. It doesn't help that in our victim-shaming world, people make it more uncomfortable because they blame the victim involved. Rape becomes an even harder and more complicated discussion when the victim knows their attacker, is close or intimately involved with them, or has somehow had a formalized relationship with that person. For those who are unsure of what I am talking about, welcome to the world of date rape.

84% of women who are raped knew their attacker prior to the assault. 57% of rapes occur while a woman is on a date. If these statistics aren't shocking enough, the realities behind them are more staggering. 25% of men believe rape is acceptable if the woman asked out the man, the man pays for things on the date, or the woman returns to an intimate setting with a man after a date. 33% of surveyed males said they would commit an act of rape if they believed they could get away with it. 84% of males who committed acts that met with the legal definition of rape refused to believe they had done anything wrong whatsoever, and only 25-30% of women whose sexual assault experiences met the legal definition of rape considered themselves to be rape victims. 50% of high school boys and 42% of high school girls believe there are instances where it is acceptable for a male to hold down a female and physically force her into sexual acts.[33] Those are some facts that need to sink in for a long time as we ponder on the messages we are sending our young people about power and control as pertains to sex and sexuality.

We always tell our girls to beware the strangers that lurk in dark corners and the strangers who have candy, but we often fail to realize that the most powerful and destructive enemies might come in the form of attentive boyfriends or husbands, people who seem to take an interest in them with the goal of violating them. Because of the connection many women have to their rapists or sexual assailants, they don't consider what happened to them to be rape or violation – they just think it's a part of a dating experience. This is particularly damaging and serious for our young women, whose experiences with dating are limited and can easily think that such an experience is normal or desirable.

Somewhere in here, we must stand up as a society and make it clear that rape is unacceptable, no matter who a rapist might be to a rape victim. In addition to educating our girls, we need to take a stand and educate our boys in respect for women and respect for others in a dating situation. These statistics need to alert us to the fact that our young men and women need education in self-control, respect for the boundaries of others, and a general sense of maturity and honor before they ever take to the game of social or serious relationships.

- DAILY DISCIPLINE: VOLUNTEER AT AN ORGANIZATION THAT SPECIALIZES IN RAPE AND SEXUAL ASSAULT.

- DAY 96 -
Racism: Alive and Thriving

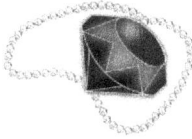

PETER BEGAN TO SPEAK [OPENED HIS MOUTH]: "I REALLY [TRULY]
UNDERSTAND NOW THAT TO GOD EVERY PERSON IS THE SAME
[GOD DOES NOT SHOW FAVORITISM/PARTIALITY]."
(ACTS 10:34)

- DAILY READING: REVELATION 7:9-17

In 2012, a neo-Nazi went into a Wisconsin Sikh temple and opened fire. He killed six people and wounded three others. In 2014, a married couple who was a part of an anti-establishment organization, shot two police officers in a Las Vegas pizzeria. They left a swastika on the bodies of the dead officers, a flag with the words "Don't tread on me" and a note that said, "This is the start of the revolution." They then went and killed someone at a Wal-Mart.[34]

The media sends us the message we should fear immigrants and radical individuals of other countries, but seldom do we receive the message that there are plenty of disconcerting values born and bred in the United States on their own. White supremacy is a topic that most think of in a bygone era, in the "deep south," during post-slavery days in rural America. Many are surprised to know that since September 11, 2001, almost twice as many people have died due to acts of white supremacists and other non-Muslim extremists than by what we now classify as "radical Muslims."[35] Since the year 2000, the number of hate groups operating in the United States has increased 54%.[36] We don't typically hear about their crimes on the national news, but it doesn't change the truth that white supremacist groups, fueled with hate, music that reinforces hate, and many times drugs such as methamphetamines are alive and well, busy recruiting young people and insisting that America would be better if there was no diversity present therein.

It should concern all of us that racism is such a dominating force in the images many have of American ideology and patriotism. It is not uncommon to find under flag-waving individuals a broiling seat of hate, desiring to purify the United States in one form or another. Even though the extremes of racism might not always take the form of thinking other races should be killed or exterminated, there are many who feel that different races should assimilate into white culture, adopting white custom and attitude, and that those who do not are in some semblance refusing to be American.

It's foolish and ignorant to deny the reality that American culture was built upon ideals that are less-than-Christian. Slavery, sexism, vices (tobacco and alcohol), secret societies, and hidden, less-than-altruistic ideals are the very fiber of American being, the very things that were built upon to bring the wealth of this nation into center stage. America became an international superpower by exploiting and using free labor and marginalizing the original settlers who lived here. The longer we keep trying to skirt around these issues or pretend that they aren't real or not relevant to today, the longer it will take us, as a nation, to begin the healing that must start.

Some things are just not acceptable for those who claim to be Christian. Espousing racist values is one of them. That's the beginning and the ending of that whole matter.

- DAILY DISCIPLINE: MAKE A POINT TO WORSHIP WITHIN DIVERSITY.

- DAY 97 -
Violent Faith

SINCE THE TIME [FROM THE DAYS] JOHN THE BAPTIST CAME UNTIL NOW, THE KINGDOM OF HEAVEN HAS BEEN GOING FORWARD IN STRENGTH [ADVANCING FORCEFULLY; OR SUBJECT TO VIOLENCE; SUFFERING VIOLENT ATTACKS], AND FORCEFUL [OR VIOLENT] PEOPLE HAVE BEEN TRYING TO TAKE IT BY FORCE [LAY HOLD OF IT; OR ATTACK IT].
(MATTHEW 11:12)

- DAILY READING: MATTHEW 11:7-15

Christian history is wrought with individuals who have mixed church and state. The Crusades, the Holy Roman Empire, the peasant revolts of the Reformation, and the rest of the long and complicated wars show people who were interested in using the church to advance their own causes of world domination and power. The history of the church shows us that those who used the most physical force often got what they wanted and shaped the history of nations, individuals, and yes, even denominations, at least for a time.

Both church and world history alike show us the powerful way violence influences events and changes the face of lives and nations. It is seldom positive and always shows up as a force to be reckoned with. Much of the New Testament advocates peaceful solutions and a retreat from secular force rather than encouraging it. So, one might ask the question, what does a verse such as "the violent take it by force" even have in place within the Scriptures?

There are many ways this passage is interpreted, and scholars do not universally agree on the underlying tone therein. There are some who think the Kingdom of God would be taken by force by those who are violent, and there are others who believe the passage speaks of a "violent faith" and a need to be "violent" in our faith. I believe both interpretations lend credibility to the passage, and we need to pay attention both to those who try to seize their way into the Kingdom of God and be people who see to it that our faith is ready and waiting to serve its purpose in its time.

If we are to be people who have a "violent faith" that means we should aggressively seek the things of God and of faith in all that we do. We should look for and seek opportunities to do good and to live out our faith in our lives. Instead of sitting back and hoping things will change or get better on their own, we should be actively doing and looking for the chance to spread our faith by doing everything we are called to do. The Christian faith is a complete walk, something that gives us the consistent challenge to do and be better than we were yesterday.

A violent faith calls us to be motivated people who desire the things of God more than we desire the power of this world. That means the way we walk in our faith might be different from the aggression of this world, but we should pursue it just as intensely and with the same fervor as those seeking worldly aspirations and powers. Giving others the chance to experience what God has for them because we do and live right is better than watching any earthly leader take power or any battle be won.

There is an eternal fight that has no earthly solution. It will never be solved with physical violence. It will never be won with earthly battles. A violent faith may not resemble the churches of this world, but it will always imitate the things of God.

- DAILY DISCIPLINE: ACTIVATE YOUR FAITH AND USE IT AS A MOTIVATOR TO DO GOOD THINGS IN YOUR LIFE.

- DAY 98 -
Now You See Them…Soon, You Won't

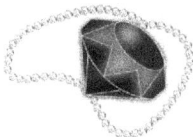

THE PEOPLE OF THE EARTH HAVE RUINED [DEFILED] IT, BECAUSE THEY DO
NOT FOLLOW [HAVE VIOLATED/TRANSGRESSED] GOD'S TEACHINGS
[THE LAWS/INSTRUCTION; TORAH] OR OBEY GOD'S LAWS
[STATUTES; REGULATIONS] OR KEEP THEIR AGREEMENT WITH GOD
THAT WAS TO LAST FOREVER [THE ETERNAL COVENANT/TREATY].
(ISAIAH 24:5)

• DAILY READING: GENESIS 1:20-25

I was delighted to see several headlines that celebrate a few well-known endangered species were finally off the endangered list. In the process, however, I learned about an endangered species I had never considered: freshwater mussels. Providing essential purpose to aquatic ecosystems, mussels stand as filter feeders (cleaning the water). They also excrete nutrients and aid in micro-organism growth that feed fish and other aquatic beings. Because of the way they live in the bottom of rivers, streams, and lakes, they are vulnerable to changes, such as flooding, droughts, or pollution.[37] The result is a serious, notable endangerment among the freshwater mussel population.

Discussion of endangered species is seldom on the lips of preachers. I'd venture it's probably not something a lot of Christians think about, because it is something we haven't been trained to consider. We also don't, as a rule, look around every day and think about the various species that no longer exist. Even though we aren't seeing them with our own eyes, endangerment and extinction are two very real realities that are changing the face of the planet as we know it. Climate changes, poaching, killing animals for hides, tusks, or other body parts on the black market, game hunting, shrinking habitats, pollution and dumping are all creating an atmosphere that is unhealthy for animals and threatening their futures as a species.

Wildlife endangerment and extinction relates to how close a

species is to existing no more. As of this moment, at least 801 animal species have gone extinct. There are 3,789 animals that are critically endangered, 5,689 that are endangered, 10,002 that are vulnerable, and 4,389 that are near threatened.[38] Among some species, there are only a handful of animals left. As many as 30 to 50% of all species are heading toward extinction by the middle of this century. While extinction is a process that happens at a natural rate of about one to five species per year, dozens of species go extinct daily.[39]

It's obvious through the current state of extinction that we are not properly caring for nor respecting the creation of God in the way we should be. The Scriptures are full of instances where animals were cared for by those who tended to them. We are not here to destroy the planet and then go on our merry way. Such destruction is contrary to Scriptural principle and defies the concepts that people would have had in Biblical times. Animals were, in many ways, the backbone of ancient economies, serving as plows, transportation, machinery and assistance, and caring properly for animals meant future generations could have them as an inheritance.

Extinction is a severe hit for the earth, for our ecosystems, and for the destruction of life systems that are here for a purpose. Instead of forgetting about the losses, remember that extinction is permanent and we won't have a second chance to bring that species back. Respect the earth. Care for it. Love the wildlife that is here. Most of all, love the Creator who has endowed us with it all.

- DAILY DISCIPLINE: GO FOR A WALK IN A NATURE PRESERVE OR PARK TO SEE THE GRANDEUR OF WILDLIFE.

- DAY 99 -
Changing our Jealous Worldview

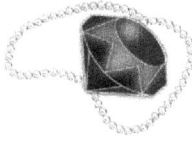

YOU MUST NOT WANT TO TAKE [COVET] YOUR NEIGHBOR'S HOUSE.
YOU MUST NOT WANT [COVET] HIS WIFE OR HIS MALE OR FEMALE SLAVES,
OR HIS OX OR HIS DONKEY, OR ANYTHING THAT BELONGS TO YOUR
NEIGHBOR [THIS COMMANDMENT INTERNALIZES PREVIOUS COMMANDMENTS].
(EXODUS 20:17)

- DAILY READING: 1 CORINTHIANS 3:1-9

*J*ealousy. We've all been there, right? Don't act all innocent; we haven't got time for that. There has been that moment in time where you cast your eyes at someone who had the relationship you wanted or the car or outfit you desired. Jealousy is often slanted in almost a "cutesy" way, making it sound like it is something that's not that serious or that bad, something that we have because we're human and it just goes along with being human. In many instances, jealousy is spoken of as something that's of particular issue for females. Women are portrayed as being jealous and envious of one another, never satisfied, and malcontented.

If we think about images of women in the media, this is just the way women are often portrayed. I've been a vocal critic of reality television because of the way it portrays women. Reality shows display the worst, rather than the best, in female behavior. Women fight over men, get into hair-pulling expeditions in public over suggestions of things or things that turn up missing, accusations run wild, and the catty, jealous behavior of the women on the programs echoes of the things people always accuse women of doing. It disturbs me greatly when I see young girls emulate the same behaviors, mannerisms, and attitudes of women on these programs, because that's what is teaching them to be women. From watching reality television, women and girls alike get the message that it's all right to be jealous, venomous, and vindictive.

If you are a Christian, none of the things I just mentioned are acceptable behaviors. We've all had our jealous moments, but God has called us to come out of that place and learn to be happy for and celebrate others. There are so many things about the lives of other people that we don't know and will never be able to assess by looking at them on the surface, and maybe that's why jealousy is such a serious problem from the Christian perspective. Jealousy assesses things from a surface-deep perspective. Just because someone appears to be happy or to have it all on the surface doesn't mean they really do, and it's very possible that the price they pay to have that surface-perfect life is higher and harder than anything we could imagine.

Not to mention, jealousy is a complete waste of time. All the energy and effort you spend wanting and yearning and pining for what someone else has could be channeled into doing something productive and making your own life become the very thing you desire it to be. God calls us to work with others and to build the Kingdom, and sitting around, worrying about what someone else has that you want is going to make sure the Kingdom takes that much longer to build. Wasting time is contrary to our purpose here, and jealousy is definitely something that wastes time.

Jealousy is one of those funny things that when you take the time to look back on, you often wonder why you spent so much time on it to begin with. It's a lot easier to avoid it all together. Life is too short to spend it hating on someone else.

- DAILY DISCIPLINE: INSTEAD OF BEING JEALOUS, EXTEND YOURSELF TO SOMEONE IN FRIENDSHIP.

- DAY 100 -
Oaks of Righteousness

THEN THEY WILL BE CALLED TREES OF GOODNESS [OR OAKS
OF RIGHTEOUSNESS], TREES PLANTED BY THE LORD TO SHOW
HIS GREATNESS [GLORY; MANIFEST PRESENCE].
(ISAIAH 61:3)

- DAILY READING: 1 CORINTHIANS 13:8-14:1

The Scriptures compare believers to trees on several occasions. There were several reasons for this. The most obvious reason was the Bible was written in an agricultural society where cultivation of trees would have been readily understood. Not everyone in ancient times had received the same level of education and would, therefore, be unfamiliar with things that pertained to the rich and powerful. When God wanted to get a message across to His people, He was careful to make sure the imagery used would be easily understood by everyone. Trees were familiar to everyone, so trees were used. The cultivation of trees, whether of fruit, for firewood, or for building, all required extensive process. In the case of fruit, a farmer had to learn how long a tree would grow before producing fruit. For the record, that process typically took years. Fruit trees are also notoriously fussy, requiring just the right conditions to get the right fruit. If a tree was used for firewood or building, it had to grow to a certain point and then experience some sort of additional treatment to serve its usable purpose.

To talk about being "oaks of righteousness" merits a special attention to details. The "oak trees" mentioned in this Bible verse aren't the oak trees as we know them in the United States, so erase any pictures of American oaks from your thinking. The tree mentioned is actually a terebinth tree, which is mentioned in a few places within the Old Testament. These "oaks of righteousness" were recognized as being as old as time itself and even though they were not often very tall, they were full-bodied, and the fruit of the tree was used in some specialty dishes. There was something special about these trees that inspired attention to eternity, to the promises of God and to a notion that all would be right within the world one day.

By calling upon us to be as "oaks of righteousness," God is calling us to remain steadfast. It's easy to be so changeable in this world that we lose our footing and people can't positively identify what we really stand for. It's appealing to chase after the things that sound good to the ears and make us want to believe they are really true. God calls us to do something else, though, and that's remain steadfast, consistent in righteousness. When people see us and see our work, they should see a piece of eternity because what we are doing touches the heart of eternity.

I've heard it said that what we do for ourselves will die with us, but what we do for someone else will last forever. There's some truth in this because even Scripture tells us the three things that will remain are faith, hope, and love, with the greatest of those three being love. If God is love and we live in love, then what we do touches others with the grace and power of God. They meet God in a way they never would have expected to do so, and their lives are changed for the better. Yeah, we need to be more steadfast, more secure. Not to mention more righteous, because righteousness shows interest and action in the things of God.

- DAILY DISCIPLINE: SEE THROUGH AN IDEA THAT YOU HAVE CHANGED YOUR MIND ABOUT SEVERAL TIMES.

- REFERENCES -

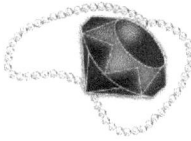

First Page quotes:
[1]"Every Small Step Makes A Difference."
http://www.sapphyr.net/peace/peace-quotes.htm. Accessed January 23, 2017.

---

[1]Marino, Lee Ann B. "The Proverbs 31 Woman: Celebrating The Blessing That Is Woman." *Most Blessed Among All Women*. Raleigh, North Carolina: Photini Press, 2017. Page 120.

[2]"Pearl." https://en.wikipedia.org/wiki/Pearl. Accessed January 16, 2017.

[3]The Hunger Project. http://www.thp.org/knowledge-center/know-your-world-facts-about-hunger-poverty/. Accessed July 13, 2016.

[4]How many people die of thirst every year? https://www.quora.com/How-many-people-die-of-thirst-every-year. Accessed August 2, 2016.

[5]"How Many People Experience Homelessness?"
http://nationalhomeless.org/factsheets/How_Many.html. Accessed August 8, 2016.

[6]"History of Prisons." http://www.prisonhistory.net/prison-history/history-of-prisons/. Accessed August 9, 2016.

[7]"A Quick Question: What Percentage Of Pastors Are Female?"
http://hirr.hartsem.edu/research/quick_question3.html. Accessed August 16, 2016.

[8]"Infant Mortality."
http://www.cdc.gov/reproductivehealth/MaternalInfantHealth/InfantMortality.htm. Accessed August 16, 2016.

[9]"Maternal Mortality."
http://www.who.int/mediacentre/factsheets/fs348/en/. Accessed August 16, 2016.

[10]Breyer, Melissa. "25 Shocking Fashion Industry Statistics." http://www.treehugger.com/sustainable-fashion/25-shocking-fashion-industry-statistics.html. Accessed August 16, 2016.

[11]"Grace." http://www.equalitynow.org/campaigns/trafficking-survivor-stories/grace. Accessed September 4, 2016.

[12]"Human Trafficking." https://www.unodc.org/unodc/en/human-trafficking/what-is-human-trafficking.html. Accessed September 4, 2016.

[13]"The Facts." https://polarisproject.org/facts. Accessed September 4, 2016.

[14]"11 Facts About Human Trafficking." https://www.dosomething.org/us/facts/11-facts-about-human-trafficking. Accessed September 4, 2016.

[15]"The Facts." https://polarisproject.org/facts. Accessed September 4, 2016.

[16]Marino, Lee Ann B. "Being LGBT In Society." *Ministering To LGBTs – And Those Who Love Them*. Cary, North Carolina: Righteous Pen Publications, 2016.

[17]"Facts About Bullying." http://www.stopbullying.gov/news/media/facts/index.html. Accessed September 8, 2016.

[18]"HIV/AIDS in the World." *amfAR*. https://www.amfar.org/about-hiv-aids/statistics-worldwide/. Accessed June 3, 2025.

[19]Ibid.

[20]Marino, Lee Ann B. *Compassionate Care: Healing for the Soul with HIV*. Cary, North Carolina: Apostolic University Press, 2016.

[21]Kubler-Ross, Elisabeth. *On Death And Dying*. New York, New York: Simon & Schuster, 1969.

[22]"Education Facts." http://www.compassion.com/poverty/education.htm. Accessed September 11, 2016.

[23]"11 Facts About Pollution." https://www.dosomething.org/us/facts/11-facts-about-pollution. Accessed September 11, 2016.

[24]"Oceans (Where Feet May Fail) Lyrics." Hillsong United Lyrics. http://www.metrolyrics.com/oceans-where-feet-may-fail-lyrics-hillsong-

united.html. Accessed September 11, 2016.

[25]"Difference Between Sheep And Goat." http://www.differencebetween.net/science/nature/difference-between-sheep-and-goat/. Accessed September 11, 2016.

[26]"Top 10 Christian Persecution Stories of 2011." http://www.christianpost.com/news/compass-direct-news-top-10-stories-of-2011-66584/. Accessed September 14, 2016.

[27]"Overview of Equal Opportunity." http://www.civilrights.org/equal-opportunity/overview.html. Accessed September 14, 2016.

[28]"Equal Pay And The Wage Gap." https://nwlc.org/issue/equal-pay-and-the-wage-gap/. Accessed September 14, 2016.

[29]"Ebenezer Elliot." https://en.wikipedia.org/wiki/Ebenezer_Elliott. Accessed September 19, 2016.

[30]"When Wilt Thou Save The People?" http://www.hymnary.org/text/when_wilt_thou_save_the_people. Accessed September 19, 2016.

[31]Armario, Christine. "Report: Students Don't Know Much About US History." http://www.nbcnews.com/id/43397386/ns/us_news-life/t/report-students-dont-know-much-about-us-history/. Accessed September 19, 2016.

[32]Evans, Rachel Held. "January: Valor – Will The Real Proverbs 31 Woman Please Stand Up?" *Year Of Biblical Womanhood, A*. Nashville, Tennessee: Thomas Nelson, 2012.

[33]"Facts About Date Rape." https://www.k-state.edu/media/webzine/Didyouhearyes/daterapefacts.html. Accessed September 19, 2016.

[34]Shane, Scott. "Homegrown Extremists Tied to Deadlier Toll Than Jihadists in US Since 9/11." http://www.nytimes.com/2015/06/25/us/tally-of-attacks-in-us-challenges-perceptions-of-top-terror-threat.html?_r=0. Accessed September 19, 2016.

[35]Hatchett, Keisha. "Statistics Show White Supremacy Is A Bigger Threat To the U.S. Than Radical Muslims." https://www.yahoo.com/news/statistics-show-white-supremacy-bigger-004327404.html?ref=gs. Accessed September 19, 2016.

[36]The State Of Hate: White Supremacist Groups Growing."
http://www.civilrights.org/publications/hatecrimes/white-supremacist.html.
Accessed September 19, 2016.

[37]"Secret Lives Of Mussels, The: America's Most Endangered Species!"
https://www2.usgs.gov/blogs/features/usgs_top_story/the-secret-lives-of-
mussels-americas-most-endangered-species/. Accessed September 19, 2016.

[38]"Endangered Species Statistics."
http://www.statisticbrain.com/endangered-species-statistics/. Accessed
September 19, 2016.

[39]"11 Facts About Endangered Species."
https://www.dosomething.org/us/facts/11-facts-about-endangered-species.
Accessed September 19, 2016.

- ABOUT THE AUTHOR -
Dr. Lee Ann B. Marino, Ph.D., D.Min., D.D.

THESE THAT HAVE TURNED THE WORLD UPSIDE DOWN ARE COME HITHER
ALSO.
(ACTS 17:6, KJV)

Dr. **Lee Ann B. Marino, Ph.D., D.Min., D.D**. (she/her) is "everyone's favorite theologian" leading Gen X, Millennials, and Gen Z with expertise in leadership training, queer and feminist theology, general religion, and apostolic theology. She has served in ministry since 1998 and was ordained as a pastor in 2002 and an apostle in 2010. She founded what is now Sanctuary Apostolic Fellowship Empowerment (SAFE) Ministries in 2004. Under her ministry heading Dr. Marino is founder and Overseer of Sanctuary International Fellowship Tabernacle (SIFT) (the original home of National Coming Out Sunday) and The Sanctuary Network, and Chancellor of Apostolic Covenant Theological Seminary (ACTS).

Affectionately nicknamed "the Spitfire," Dr. Marino has spent over two decades as an "apostle, preacher, and teacher" (2 Timothy 1:11), exercising her personal mandate to become "all things to all people" (1 Corinthians 9:22). Her embrace of spiritual issues (both technical and intimate) has found its home among both seekers and believers, those who desire spiritual answers to today's issues.

Dr. Marino has preached throughout the United States, Puerto Rico, and Europe in hundreds of religious services and experiences throughout the years. A history maker in her own right, she has spent over two decades in advocacy, education, and work for and within minority spiritual communities (including African American, Hispanic, and LGBTQ+). She has also served as the first woman on all-male synods, councils, and panels, as well as the first preacher or speaker welcomed of a different race, sexual orientation, or identity among diverse communities. Today, Dr. Marino's work extends to over 150 countries as she hosts the popular *Kingdom Now* podcast, which is in the top 20 percentile of all podcasts worldwide. She is also the author of over 35 books and the popular Patheos column, *Leadership on Fire*. To date, she has had five bestselling titles within their subject matter: *Understanding Demonology, Spiritual Warfare, Healing, and Deliverance: A Manual for the Christian Minister*; *Ministry School Boot Camp: Training for Helps Ministries, Appointments, and Beyond*; *Discovering Intimacy: A Journey Through the Song of Solomon*; *Fruit of the Vine: Study and Commentary on the Fruit of the Spirit*; and *Ministering to LGBTQ+ (and Those Who Love Them): A Primer for Queer Theology* (and its accompanying workbook).

As a public icon and social media influencer, Dr. Marino advocates healthy body image (curvy/full-figured), representation as a demisexual/aromantic, and albinism awareness as a model. Known to those she works with, she is a spiritual mom, teacher, leader, professor, confidant, and friend. She continues to transform, receiving new teaching, revelation, and insight in this thing we call "ministry." Through years of spiritual growth and maturity, Dr. Marino stands as herself, here to present what God has given to her for any who have an ear to hear.

For more information, visit her website at kingdompowernow.org.

www.ingramcontent.com/pod-product-compliance
Lightning Source LLC
Chambersburg PA
CBHW070844300326
41935CB00039B/1442